Tales of Tour

by

Alex Kolker

Sinister Dexter Press

Kewanee, Illinois

ISBN 1-892544-99-7

"It was a fantastic city, like one conjured up by Aladdin's magic lamp. One day I saw a humming hive of industry, with thousands of men, women, children, and dogs; next day all had disappeared, as if by magic.

It was fascinating to watch the city grow caravan by caravan, for two days before the festival the camping-ground was still empty. This city of tents and caravans sprouts like a mushroom in a night. At first the caravans arrive nonchalantly and take up their positions like outposts on the common, then the city begins gradually to grow more speedily as the caravans follow each other in quick succession.

There was as much companionship between the various carts as if they had all belonged to the same family. Not only had they all one supreme cult in common, but they had met one another on countless occasions in their nomadic peregrinations from fair to fair."

.An account of a gathering of the Roma (European gypsies), from Walter Starkie's <u>In Sara's Tents</u>

TABLE OF CONTENTS

This book is dedicated to Bill and Lenore, without whom
it would never have been started, and to Amy, without
whom it would never have been finished.

INTRODUCTION

Ever since my college days, I have been a Deadhead — one of several hundred thousand of the most dedicated fans of the rock group the Grateful Dead. Whenever the band went on tour, we would all pack up and follow along after them, getting into as many concerts as we could, and hanging out together in the concert hall parking lots before and after each show. There, we would meet, play music, and buy and sell each other's crafts, tie-dyed T-shirts, food, and drugs. I used to earn my pocket change on tour by selling bound copies of these short stories at the shows.

Jerry Garcia's death, in August of 1995, was literally the end of an era. And while nothing indeed can fully replace the Dead, tour itself has gone on — with Furthur Fests and the Other Ones, and of course Phish. Touring, then, has become more than just a Deadhead phenomenon. It has become a permanent part of American culture.

To mark this fact, I have included in this collection "The Lost Girl" — the first Tale of Tour I wrote which takes place at a Phish show rather than at a Dead show. It is the first time that this story has ever appeared in print. Let's hope that — as I continue to tour, selling these books at any Phish concert I can get to — still more Tales of Tour follow.

I would like to take this opportunity to thank the many people who helped me bring this book, finally, to print.

First and foremost is Aaron Rosenberg at Clockworks, who hooked me up with a good printer, donated his graphic design skills, and even supplied me with one of his company's ISBN numbers. As he once said about me (in print, no less) I will now say about him: he is a true friend. You can read more about Clockworks at:

http://www.clockworksgames.com/

I'd also like to thank the immensely talented Jeremy Rizza for supplying the cover drawing. My hope is that this is far from the last time one of his illustrations appears in print. You can find more examples of his work at:

http://www.jeremyrizza.com/

Third, I would also like to thank Janet Young at Lightning Print for her patience and guidance, and for taking the time to fit my little project into her much-too-busy schedule.

I'd like to thank Bill for all those fine, fun tours of years past. The fact that I have based three separate characters in this book on him shows what an inspiration he's been to me. I hope that he and I have many more tours yet to come.

Last but never least, I'd like to thank my wife Amy, who always believed in me — but, better yet, who taught me how to believe in myself.

— Alex Kolker

May 2000

DEADHEADS

James P. Rovender III's limousine is the most spacious one he'd been able to find that was, at the same time, small enough to navigate the narrow streets of downtown Chicago. Normally, the back seat was more than enough for him. But on this Friday afternoon he's forced to share with underlings: Ms. Baker, his personal secretary, and Mr. West, one of the hungry young wolves from the firm's legal department. They're on their way back into the city after a very fruitful business meeting in the north suburbs. Rovender's satisfaction at business well completed is dulled only by the presence of the two employees, but as soon as they get back to corporate headquarters he can drop them off, and then he'll have the back seat all to himself on the long drive home.

Ms. Baker — a quiet, pretty woman, just hitting middle age — has accompanied Rovender in the limo before, and she always sits demurely and respectfully, making as little of a distraction of herself as possible. Mr. West has never been in the limo before, however, and it shows. He keeps fidgeting with the buttons and dials, running his finger across the row of bottles in the wet bar, examining the television and the VCR and the copier and the FAX machine. "They're like little toys," he says, delighted. Rovender returns the young man's grin with stony derision. If West weren't such a shrewd lawyer, Rovender would have sworn to himself then and there never to take him to a business meeting again.

Just fifteen more minutes, he tells himself, as he watches West sneak yet another peppermint out of the candy dish.

Then, suddenly and without warning, the limo comes to a complete stop.

Rovender leans forward, pushing the switch that lowers the screen between the back seat and Leon, the driver. "What is it? What is it?"

"I don't know," Leon grunts. He's punching the tuner buttons of the radio with his stubby fingers. "Some sort of back-up. I'll look for a traffic report."

Rovender stares past Leon, through the windshield. The expressway stretches out before them, clotted with unmoving cars.

The old man scowls. "Try to drive through it," he orders nonsensically, and he raises the screen again.

"What is it?" Ms. Baker asks.

"Traffic," Rovender answers. "It must be some sort of accident."

"I don't think so," West says. He twists around in his seat, turning his back to Rovender, and peers out the window at the cars stalled alongside them.

"What do you mean?"

"Look at that VW microbus," West says. "Look at that RV with the tie-dye flag. There's a Grateful Dead concert at Soldier Field tonight. I bet that's what's causing all the traffic."

"These people are all going to a concert? Some sort of rock concert?"

"Yes sir."

"It's four o'clock in the afternoon!" Rovender cries out.

"I know," West says. "But for Grateful Dead concerts, the people like to show up early. You know: tailgate parties."

Rovender doesn't know the term, so he ignores it. "You mean to say that these people have nothing better to do with their time than go to some sort of rock concert in the middle of the afternoon?"

"I guess not," West answers, his nose all but pressed to the glass, staring out at the cars. At least he's stopped playing with the buttons, Rovender tells himself.

Time drags on, the traffic creeping forward a few feet every five minutes or so. All around the limo, the young people have gotten out of their cars and are standing around — right in the middle of the expressway! — chatting with one another and wandering up and down the shoulder of the road. Every once in a while one of them bends down to leer through the limo's tinted windows and tap on the glass. "Ignore them," Rovender orders sharply.

"No wonder they've brought traffic to a halt," Rovender

grumbles to himself after another twenty minutes.

"Look at them!" Rovender announces after another half an hour, startling Ms. Baker out of a light doze. "Talk about the lilies of the field! When I was their age, I was working sixty hours a week in an accounting office, and running my own investment business on the side. I worry about our country in the next fifty years, if these are the sorts of people we'll be turning it over to."

"Actually," West breaks in, turning to face Rovender, "that's not really fair. First of all, not all Deadheads are teenagers."

"Dead what?"

"Deadheads," West explains. "That's what these people call themselves."

"And how do you know that?"

West gives an uncomfortable shrug. "I knew a few of them back when I was in college."

"Where was it you went to school?"

"Stanford."

Rovender snorts and gives a slight nod.

"Not all Deadheads are teenagers," West repeats. "There are even Deadheads who are your age."

"I can imagine what pillars of the community those people must be."

"More than that," West goes on, "quite a few Deadheads have full-time, high-paying, respectable careers like we do."

"These people? Hold down jobs? Who would hire them?"

"You'd be surprised. Even Al Gore has been to a few

Grateful Dead concerts."

"He's the vice president, and a Democrat," Rovender counters, sneering. "I wouldn't exactly call that a full-time, high-paying, respectable career."

"And I mean, sure, I've met a lot of Deadheads who didn't seem to do anything for a living," West admits. "There are others who do temp work — you know: construction, waiting tables — whenever they aren't on tour. But quite a few Deadheads are fine, upstanding citizens, just like you and me. They work real jobs fifty weeks out of the year and go to these concerts on their two weeks' vacation. The kids with the long hair are easy to spot. But there are plenty of Deadheads who look just as normal — who are just as normal — as we are."

Rovender raises an eyebrow in the direction of three young men passing a hand-rolled cigarette between them right beside the limousine. "Nonsense!"

"I mean it," West returns. "Deadheads are everywhere. Everyone knows someone who's a Deadhead. You probably know more than a few of them yourself."

"I don't know anyone like this trash," Rovender insists.

"You'd be surprised."

"I'd be very surprised."

"I'll tell you what," West says. "I'll bet you twenty dollars that every person in this car knows someone who's going to the concert tonight."

Rovender casts a glance in the direction of the back of Leon's head, blocked from view behind the privacy screen.

"I wouldn't be surprised to find that my driver knew someone who was going to this concert," he says, sniffing sharply. "Now if <u>Ms. Baker</u> knew someone going to the concert tonight, <u>then</u> I'd be surprised."

Ms. Baker, on hearing her name, snaps into focus. "Sir?"

"Is it a bet?" Rovender asks West.

"You got it."

"Ms. Baker," Rovender says, turning to his secretary, "are you planning on attending this concert tonight?"

"Oh, no sir. Of course not."

"Do you know anyone else who's going?" West asks.

"Well . . . ." She shoots a nervous glance back at Rovender.

"Go on, Ms. Baker," Rovender assures her.

"Well, my sister's kid — I mean, my nephew, Frank — he goes to these concerts all the time. He once followed the band around the country for three whole months."

West clears his throat, holding out his hand. Rovender's mouth twists as he pulls a twenty out of his billfold and drops it into West's palm. "A black sheep nephew — that was just a lucky break," the old man grumbles.

West glances at his watch. "Want to go double or nothing?"

Rovender squints at the young man. "What's the bet?"

"I'll bet you double or nothing that <u>you</u> know someone who's going to this concert too."

"<u>Me</u>? That's impossible."

"We have a bet then?"

"Certainly."

West glances at his watch again, and then starts tugging loose his tie. "It's five. I'm off the clock. So I guess I'll just find my own way home."

"What do you mean, you —?"

West smiles and reaches into his jacket pocket, pulling out a long strip of colored cardboard — a concert ticket. "I'll get that other twenty from you bright and early Monday morning, sir." And with that, he drops his tie into his briefcase, pushes open the door to the limo and, tugging off his jacket, steps out onto the expressway with the rest of the concert-goers.

"Wait —" Rovender objects, but West neatly shuts the door behind him.

"It is five o'clock, sir," Ms. Baker says, her voice wavering a little.

"We're still miles away from the stadium," Rovender notes, turning around in his seat to watch West walk up to and join a group of scraggly teenagers by the side of the road. "How does he expect to get to his concert? How does he expect to get home?"

Ms. Baker shrugs. "Maybe he'll just hitch a ride. My nephew does it all the time. It drives my sister crazy."

Rovender turns forward in his seat again, breathes in sharply, and stiffens his spine. "Ms. Baker?"

"Yes, Mr. Rovender?"

"Please make a note to arrange for a drug urine test for Mr. West bright and early Monday morning."

15

"Yes sir."

The old man clears his throat and stares sourly out the limousine window.

ACE SCORES A TICKET

The easiest part is getting the ride to Buffalo in the first place. All Ace has to do is hike five miles down to the highway rest area, and hitch along with the first Heads passing through who look halfway decent. He ends up with Benny and Pete, two high schoolers from California with a tank of pharmaceutical nitrous in the trunk. Pete insists, every hundred miles or so, that the three of them stop and sample the wares. When they drop Ace off at Rich Stadium — vacant and desolate — early the next morning, he has a sore throat and a mild headache, and his mind is slow and wasted. He staggers over to the edge of a nearby field and sleeps for a few hours in a clump of bushes.

When he wakes up, it's just past noon. His skin is tight and dry on the side of his face that was facing up to the sun while he slept. The other side of his face is wet with summer soil. The parking-lot scene is already underway, having sprung up around him while he slept: running children, barking dogs, venders and customers, jewelry and T-shirts, the distant rhythms of a drum circle, and not a security guard in sight.

He stumbles out of the field and down the dirt road

that runs along one side of the stadium complex, towards two buildings in the distance. One of them is just a gas station, but the other one turns out to be a restaurant, and Ace ducks inside. Most of the customers are Heads, so no one notices Ace, in his own tie-dye and cut-off shorts, as he sneaks through the restaurant and into the bathroom.

He runs the water in the sink for a full minute to get it nice and hot, and then rinses his face and hair thoroughly. He takes off his shirt, dries off with it, and puts it back on again. Then he scrubs his teeth clean with his index finger, sprinkles a few drops of cold water across his face for good measure, and leaves the bathroom.

When he tries to sneak back out of the restaurant again, however, a huge man in an apron appears in front of him, cutting him off at the front door. "Restrooms for customers only."

"Oh wow. Sorry, man," Ace says, in his best druggie burn-out voice. "I didn't know."

The man — a small plastic pin identifies him as the restaurant manager — grabs Ace by the scruff of the neck and leads him over to a big sign by the restroom door: RESTROOMS FOR CUSTOMERS ONLY.

"Now," the manager asks, "what would you like to order, sir?"

"I'm really not hungry —"

"A cup of coffee's fifty cents," the manager says, his grip on Ace's neck tightening. "A slice of pie is a dollar."

"Coffee and pie would be great."

"Sit down, sir, and your breakfast will be along shortly."

And with that, the manager lets him go. The back of Ace's neck tingles and sparks. "Well, then," he calls out to the manager's retreating back, "you can just forget about your tip."

"Damn hippies," the manager mumbles to himself, settling back into his seat by the cash register.

Ace sits at an empty table, digging through his pockets and his fanny pack for any change he can find. He comes up with a little over two dollars. He's about to lose three-fourths of his money, and he hasn't even gotten to the scene yet.

He passes the time by pouring the salt into the sugar jar and the sugar into the salt shaker. When the coffee and pie comes, Ace mashes the pie into a shapeless grey mass, inverts the full coffee cup on the saucer, and bends all the silverware into knots. He drops a dollar-fifty on the table, waits until the manager is busy harassing someone else, and then slips quietly out of the restaurant.

He dives immediately into the nearest clot of Heads, and walks with them straight into the scene. The parking lots are already more than half full. The sun is bright but not too hot. A light wind fans Ace's face without kicking up too much dust from the road. It's going to be a great day.

There aren't any cops around, at least not as far as Ace can see, so everyone is cool and relaxed. The venders are out in full force, selling openly. Ace even spots an acid dealer walking around with a big sign reading CHEAP TRIPS.

When the vending is this free and easy, it really picks up the energy of the scene. The Rich Stadium parking lots look more like an Arabian bazaar. Venders zip through the slow-moving crowd, filling the air with hawker's cries.

"Brownies! Yummy brownies!"

"Kind veggie bumper stickers!"

"Juice and soda!"

"Trade tomorrow for tonight!"

"Busch, Busch Lite, and Molson Gold! Right here!"

Ace pauses at the edge of the crowd, standing cross-armed, watching it all with a big smile on his face. "Capitalism in its purest form," he mutters to himself proudly.

He stops a passing Head wearing a wristwatch. "What time is it, brother?"

"Two," the Head tells him.

Four hours, Ace thinks to himself. That should be more than enough time.

He spots a Deadhead selling fruit juice out of a styrofoam cooler on one side of the aisle. He strolls up to him, hanging his head a little, trying to look as hot and sweaty as possible. "Hey, man."

"Hey," the vender grunts.

"Look," Ace says. "I don't got enough money to buy a juice from you, but I'd kill for some ice to suck on. Could you spare some?"

"No way, man. You want to drink something, you pay for it!"

Shit, Ace thinks to himself as he walks away. First the restaurant manager, and now this guy. Two assholes in a row. Bad Karma.

He follows the flow of traffic further down the aisle until he finds another vender with a cooler — this one full of soda. Ace asks him for a piece of ice.

"Sure," the vender replies, his fingers already fishing through the water for a cube. He comes up with several, and hands them over to Ace with a smile. Ace smiles back, and slips away into the crowd.

He finds a secluded spot, and then reaches down and unties the woven bracelet from around his ankle. He bought it only a few weeks ago, so it hasn't really started to unravel yet. Rubbing it with one of the ice cubes, he works all of the dust and sweat out from the weave of the threads. The water even makes the colors deeper and brighter. When he's got what looks to be a brand new bracelet, he tosses what's left of the ice under a parked car and steps out into the flow of the crowd.

"Who wants my last bracelet?" he calls out. "I've sold a hundred and ninety-nine bracelets so far on tour. This is my very last one."

After five minutes, he finds a taker. "Your last one?" the Head asks.

"Yeah," Ace says. "I wish now I'd made twice as many as I did."

"It's pretty cool," the Head says, examining it. "How much?"

"Two."

"Okay. Let's do it." He hands Ace two bills and Ace hands him the bracelet. "Hey," the Head asks. "Why is it wet?"

"Some asshole got me with a squirt gun earlier."

"Oh yeah. They got me the other day. I hate that."

"Water dries," Ace tells him with a shrug.

Ace wanders back down the dirt road, to the gas station next to the restaurant. He gets eight quarters from the station attendant, who's already looking a little harried by all the Deadheads swarming around — buying gas, shoplifting munchies, waiting in line to use the pay phone. Ace buys four sodas from the vending machine around the back, takes off his shirt and wraps them up in it, and carries them back to the scene.

"Ice cold soda! Freezing cold! Soda for a buck!" It takes him only a few minutes to sell all four.

Just as he's making his last sale, he spots a vender with a table set up on one side of the aisle. He's selling mostly silver-wire jewelry and tumbled stones, but what catches Ace's eye is a basket of woven bracelets with a sign reading ONE DOLLAR.

Ace comes up to the booth. "How's it going, brother?"

"Great!" the vender answers. "I haven't had a selling day like this in years."

"I know what you mean."

Ace buys four of the bracelets. He ties the best one to his ankle, to replace the one he sold earlier. He wanders

22

through the crowd hawking the other three for two dollars each. It takes longer for him to unload the bracelets than it did for him to sell the soda, but at least he doesn't have to make the ten minute trek to and from the gas station.

When he finally sells the third bracelet, he goes back to the same booth and buys six more. The vender gives him a funny look, but doesn't say anything.

Ace takes it much more slowly now. Six bracelets are going to take a while to sell no matter what he does, so there's no need to push his sales pitch or to race all over the lots. He comes across a woman in tie-dye and beads playing old Joni Mitchell tunes on a beat-up guitar, and he joins the crowd around her to listen for a while. He takes part in a few rounds of hackey-sack, and sells a bracelet to one of the players. He bums a cigarette off another Head, and stands a few minutes in the shade of a tour bus, smoking and watching the scene race by him. He trades two of the bracelets for a cheap piece of crystal on a leather thong, and then sells the necklace to someone else for five dollars.

After an hour, he sells the last bracelet, and heads back to the booth for more.

"Didn't you already buy some of these?" the vender asks, squinting up at him.

"Must've been somebody else," Ace assures him. "Some other guy in long hair and tie dye."

"No, it was you, man," the vender insists. "Son of a bitch. You've been reselling my merchandise!"

"What do you care? You got the price you're asking for."

23

"Well," the vender says. "My price just went up." He reaches over, snatches away the ONE DOLLAR sign, and rips it cleanly in half.

"Whatever," Ace says, and he leaves. Bracelets are too tough a sell anyway. And what does that guy care what happens to his bracelets after he sells them? He could sell them for two bucks apiece himself if he was willing to do some hustling, instead of sitting on his ass all day.

Ace counts the money in his pocket. He's got thirteen dollars and fifty cents. Not quite enough.

He finds a vender selling six-packs of beer for ten dollars. Ace buys one, wraps it up in his shirt, and sells the individual cans for two dollars apiece. These go pretty quick, but the profit is too small. Still, he has fifteen dollars now — enough to start wandering around with a finger up in the air.

He passes by a kid — she can't be more than thirteen years old — selling home-made tie-dyes for five dollars each. Ace stands watching her, considering this new product. These are the old-style, rubber band, concentric circle tie-dyes, but each shirt has at least two colors of ink in them, which is a nice touch. They don't seem to be selling all that well, but then again the kid isn't really into it. Ace, with his hard-working hard sell, might be able to unload a few of them for eight dollars apiece.

Finally he gives in, and buys two.

It turns out to be a mistake. He hustles for forty-five minutes before he can sell the first one. There are just too many of the modern-style fire-dyes on the lots. He hustles the second T-shirt for half an hour, and then finally just hooks it in his belt and wanders off looking for a more lucrative product.

He buys and then resells another six pack of beer, bringing his money back up to fifteen dollars and fifty cents. He's still got one finger up in the air, but so do half the other Heads in the lot. It's going to be harder to find a ticket than he thought.

Next he comes across a Deadhead selling packs of cigarettes for two dollars apiece. He must have bought a whole crate of cigarettes at bulk rate, or maybe he just shoplifted a carton — otherwise he wouldn't be making a profit at that price. But Heads are used to paying a little extra for the things they buy on the lots. Ace buys seven packs, and quickly resells them for three dollars each. Cigarettes practically sell themselves. In the end, all Ace has to do is walk around with a pack held high in the air, and the customers come to him.

When all else fails in the world of sales, Ace muses to himself, you can always count on people's addictions. The best product, of course, is drugs. Ace could have made all of the money he's made today ten times over, and in half the time, if he'd been dealing acid instead of bracelets and cigarettes. But Ace wants to see the show tonight — not the inside of a holding cell.

He finds a woman selling grilled cheese sandwiches for two dollars apiece and buys one. He washes it down with a one-dollar soda, and then sits down to digest for a while in the crowd at the edge of a drum circle. This is a really good group of drummers. They pound and beat their little hearts out, letting the rhythm lead them, rather than them leading the rhythm. To one side, a whole line of Heads sit shaking strings of tiny silver anklet bells, which adds a light, magical quality to the percussion. There's also a girl playing a tambourine. But she isn't just beating on the damn thing — she really knows how to play one. In her hands, it comes alive. Every time she shakes it, it sends off a crystal shower of pure sound.

Ace could sit there listening for hours. But he still has business to conduct. He finally tears himself away and heads back into the main flow of the crowd.

He's within reach of his goal, now. All he needs is one more good, lucrative product and he should have enough for a ticket. He wanders back and forth through the lots, considering carefully. Finally, he hits paydirt. He catches sight of two venders selling tie-dyes just twenty yards down the aisle from one another. One is selling them out of a backpack for ten dollars each, while the other, his merchandise laid out on a tarp, is selling his tie-dyes for twelve.

Ace buys a ten-dollar shirt from the backpack vender. He has the man go deep down into his pack to make sure that the shirt Ace buys is the best one the man has to offer. Then Ace melts back into the crowd, standing to one side, watching. He waits until, through the natural ebb and flow of the crowd, the backpack vender is surrounded by customers and the other vender's tarp is not, and then Ace steps up to the tarp.

"Hey, brother. How's business?"

"Okay."

"Well, I thought you should know that guy down the aisle there is selling his dyes for ten bucks apiece," Ace tells him, pointing. "He's making a killing."

The vender stares off in the direction of the other vender, but then shakes his head. "My business is going just fine."

"Okay, brother. It's your nickel," Ace says, turning to look back at the other vender, who's still lost in the middle of a mob of potential customers. "I just wanted you to know that he's been raking it in like that all afternoon. Hand over fist. Look at the shirt he sold me." Then, with a small flourish, he shows the vender the shirt he bought.

"Nice shirt," is all the vender will say. Ace smiles, and wanders off; there's nothing to do now but wait.

When he comes back, five minutes later, the second vender has dropped the price of his shirts to eight dollars apiece. Ace buys one, carries both of his shirts over to the other side of the lot, and sells them both for twelve each. He zips back over, buys three more eight-dollar shirts, and resells them as well.

He makes a quick count of the lump of bills crumpled into the front pocket of his fanny-pack. He now has thirty-seven dollars. Paydirt.

It takes him twenty minutes to find the dealer with the

CHEAP TRIPS sign. Just the fact that this guy wasn't arrested hours ago shows how loose the scene has been today. "How much?" Ace asks him.

"Five for fifteen."

"How much for two?"

"Eight."

"Seven?"

"Eight."

"Come on. Please, man. Can't you make it seven?"

The dealer smiles, shaking his head. "Okay, man. Seven."

Ace buys two hits and drops them immediately. Then, his work nearly done, he saunters over to the front gate to check out the going price for resold tickets.

There are fewer Heads out selling tickets than Ace had expected. The low supply means a big demand, and higher prices. He finally finds one seller who's more or less in his price range.

"Twenty-five," Ace offers.

"Oh, come on, man," the Head complains. "That's face, man. I've got to make some profit on this."

Ace suppresses a sneer — not good for business. "It's not even a very good seat," he counters. "And the show starts in fifteen minutes. You'll be lucky if you get twenty."

"Thirty-five. That's my price."

"Come on, man. All I got is thirty."

"Can't do it, man."

"I swear to God," Ace says. "Look." He starts digging

28

through his pockets, coming up with his spare change. "Thirty dollars and fifty-three cents. It's all the money I've got."

"Sorry."

Just then Ace remembers the bulge at his hip. It's the homemade tie-dye he bought from the kid hours ago. "How about thirty and a shirt?"

The Head takes the shirt, examining it carefully — checking the size and the brand name, checking the seams for loose threads. A real expert. "Sure," he says, finally. "What the hell?"

In another second, the deal is made, and Ace strides over to the crowd trickling through the main gate. He glows with the satisfaction of a job well done.

Finally, he gets up to the turnstile and hands over his ticket. But the security guard stops him before he can push his way through.

"Sorry," the guard says. "It's counterfeit."

"What?"

"The ticket. It's a fake."

"Oh, come on, man. You've got to be joking."

But the guard's only answer is to shake his head.

"Come on, man. I spent thirty bucks on that ticket."

"Next time, buy it from the box office," the guard tells him. "Now clear out."

It takes ten minutes for Ace to work his way back through the crowd into the open parking lot.

"That son of a bastard," he grumbles, fuming. "I'll

counterfeit him."

But, of course, by the time he gets back to where he bought the fake ticket, the scalper is long gone.

"All that time," Ace mumbles to himself, as he kicks and shuffles his way back to the gate. "All that time. All that work. And I get fooled by some damn kid with a fake ticket. I can't fucking believe it."

The area around the gate is swarming with Deadheads, each of them with a finger up in the air. Ace peers wearily at them, and then just sinks down on the curb, his head in his hands.

Oh well, he thinks to himself. It's been a long time since I've dosed out on the lots. And this has been such a cool scene, maybe there'll be some action on the lots during the show. Maybe that drum circle will still be going . . . .

These thoughts, as sincere as they are, do little to cheer him up. He leans back on his elbows now, a sour expression across his face. His eyes follow the ticket-holders swarming past him towards the gates, as they wade through the sea of miracle-seekers.

After a few minutes, a Deadhead steps up to Ace from out of the crowd. "Are you okay, brother?" he asks.

Ace squints up at the man. He looks to be in his early thirties. His clothes are just as ratty as those of every other Head in the lot — except for the shoes, which (Ace can't help noticing) are new and expensive. You can always tell by the shoes.

"Yeah, I guess."

"Aren't you going into the show?"

Ace sighs, and shakes his head. "My ticket was a fake."

"Tough luck," the man says, squatting down next to Ace. "But that's the risk you take when you buy your ticket out here on the lot. There are lots of grifters at the scene."

"Tell me about it," Ace grumbles.

"Why aren't you looking for a miracle ticket?"

Ace dismisses the suggestion with a wave of his hand. "I've never been comfortable with begging for tickets like that. If I can't pay good hard cash, then I just put it down to karma and leave it at that."

"Admirable," the Head says, nodding.

"No one ever gets miracles anymore anyway," Ace adds. "Tickets are too hot a commodity these days just to give them away."

"Unless you're a millionaire."

"Right. And how many millionaires are there on the lots?"

"Not many, I imagine."

Ace glances back down at the Head's shoes, and then at the odd smile on the man's face.

"I really wanted to get into the show, too," Ace says, keeping his voice light and casual. "It's the only show I could make this tour."

The man stands suddenly. "Here," he says. He pulls a small envelope out of his pocket, and offers it to Ace. Ace takes it, and he can feel that old familiar rectangle of cardboard inside.

"Hey, brother, thanks a lot," he calls out, but the man has already slipped away into the crowd.

Ace rips the envelope open. Inside is a ticket for a seat on the stadium floor — fifth row, Jerry's side. "God damn!" he mutters under his breath.

He jumps to his feet and starts to push his way through the crowd. He's three steps away from the gate before he stops himself.

Ace looks down at the envelope, then over at the line of Heads waiting anxiously for tickets. A line of fingers of all different shapes and sizes — thin, stubby, calloused, creased, battered, grimy — each of them extended towards Heaven, each one trying to summon down a miracle.

Karma.

He walks up to the Deadhead in the line with the oldest, rattiest-looking shoes and hands the envelope to him. "There you go, brother."

It takes the Head several seconds to figure out what's in the envelope. "Cool, brother," he says, hugging Ace tightly. But as the Head starts off in the direction of the gate, Ace hangs back.

"Aren't you going in too?" the Head asks.

"Nah," Ace answers, with a grin. "My ticket was a fake."

And before the Head can comment, Ace slips back into the crowd.

SIX UP

"Six up!" calls a voice from somewhere up the aisle.

Rebecca quickly drapes her two T-shirts over her arm and fixes her gaze on nothing in particular, trying to look like just another customer. Sure enough, before she's taken another ten steps she passes two crossed-arm stadium security guards in matching red golf shirts, squinting suspiciously at the crowd flowing past them.

After another three steps, she passes a Deadhead carrying a selection of stone pipes and rolling papers in a cardboard tray. "Six up, brother. Six up." Rebecca warns him. He catches sight of the guards over Rebecca's shoulder, thanks her with a nod, and quickly turns back the way he came.

There are more different kinds of authority figures out on the scene today than Rebecca has ever seen at a Dead show before: federal marshals, stadium security, undercover narcs, even uniformed policemen. For some reason they've been cracking down on venders in particular. Rebecca has already seen half a dozen Heads get their merchandise confiscated, and she's even seen one or two get themselves arrested — supposedly for vending without a license, but really just because they dared to talk back to the cop who was shaking them down.

As for herself, Rebecca has taken all of the most extreme precautions. Her pot is back at the car, safely tucked away in the back of the glove compartment. She carries around only a few shirts at a time, so if the authorities stop her they can't take away all her merchandise at once. When she manages, every once in a while, to find someone interested in buying a shirt, they make their transaction squatting between parked cars rather than standing out in the aisles, all the while keeping an eye out for the red-shirted security guards and the federal marshals in their button-down shirts and Ray-Bans. All of this keeps her safe — as safe as you can be when you're bending a few laws with so many cops around — but it also makes it almost impossible for her to sell a shirt, and selling has been bad enough this tour as it is. Another couple of scenes like this, she muses, and she might have to go home early.

Whose idea was it to have a Dead show in the middle of downtown Pittsburgh anyway? she wonders. She hates these city shows; she prefers the green grass and open country of Deer Creek or Alpine Valley. Fewer cops, less hassles, and more trees. As she continues down the aisle, fuming silently, the river of people suddenly parts in front of her. The three marshals are standing cross-armed in a semi-circle around some poor Deadhead, making him empty what looks to be four or five hundred dollars' worth of T-shirts out of his duffel and into a large plastic garbage bag. Everyone's

34

giving them a wide berth — turning back the way they came, or ducking between cars to the next aisle over.

Rebecca herself walks casually past the marshals, keeping her head down until she is safely past. She tells herself she should just move on — now that she knows where the marshals are, at least in this parking lot, it'll be safe to sell in the other aisles for at least the next ten minutes. Besides, the less she has to do with the marshals, the better. But instead she slips to the side of the aisle and out of the flow of traffic and watches from a safe distance. She feels sorry for the Deadhead. It's obvious from the look on his face that he'd love nothing more than to snatch the bag out of the marshals' hands and run, but not many Heads are willing to risk it. If you run and they catch you, you go to jail.

The marshals hassle the Deadhead for a few minutes more. "Why don't you kids get real jobs?" one of them asks. The Head knows better than to answer.

"Do your parents know where you are?" another chimes in.

When they finally leave him — his head sagging, clutching his empty duffel in one fist — Rebecca comes up to him. The color has gone out of his face, but his eyes are burning. "Did they clean you out?" she asks him.

"Everything."

"Hey," Rebecca reassures him, "it's just shirts, right? At least they didn't arrest you."

"Great," he says. "But that was one month's salary gone

in sixty seconds. Next month's rent and bills."

"I know, I know," Rebecca tells him. She reaches out to touch his arm, but she knows it's small comfort. "My name's Rebecca."

"Sam." For all the mid-July inner-city heat, a shiver runs through him.

"Sam. Here." And she wraps her arms around him, and all the tension seems to melt out of him at once.

He smells of patchouli oil and clove cigarettes. Rebecca smiles.

Now that the marshals are safely out of sight, the aisle returns to normal and the river of Deadheads starts flowing again, streaming around the two of them. A few people stop to give Sam a pat on the shoulder or a word of encouragement.

"So what are you going to do now?" Rebecca asks him, letting go of him and taking a step back. "Are you getting into the show?"

Sam shakes his head.

"Walk with me, then," Rebecca suggests, draping her shirts over one arm and touching Sam lightly on the shoulder. "Keep me company."

Sam shrugs. "I guess I don't have anything better to do."

"You really know how to make a lady feel special, don't you?" Rebecca notes.

"I'm sorry — I —"

"It's okay," Rebecca assures him. "I know what you mean."

"Actually," Sam says with a shy smile, "I'd like that."

"Cool."

The venders on either side of the aisle are opening up for business again: unrolling blankets of jewelry and T-shirts, pulling their coolers of beer and juice and soda out from under parked cars. For a while at least, it seems almost like an ordinary Dead scene again.

"So what are you selling?" he asks her.

"These." She pulls one of the shirts off her arm and holds it out in front of him. A jumble of multicolored air-brushed lines criss-cross the white surface.

"Pretty," Sam says, "but —"

Rebecca interrupts his question. "Stare at it a little harder."

Sam takes the hem of the shirt in his hands and stretches it out tight. He stares at it, squints at it. Then, all at once, he breaks into a wide smile.

"Oh, wow. I can see it now. It's Jerry's face." He looks up, beaming, and Rebecca smiles back at him. "That's really cool. You make these yourself?"

A hand settles on Rebecca's shoulder. She spins around and Sam turns with her, and they find themselves staring up into the broad, square face of a red-shirted security guard.

"Christ," Rebecca hisses under her breath.

"Look," Sam says, "why can't you leave us alone? She wasn't selling anything. She was just showing it to me."

But the guard ignores him, glaring down at Rebecca.

"Do you have a vender's license?"

"Like I'm going to spend three hundred dollars on a six-month permit when you know damned well I'm only here for the day!"

"I take it that means no?" the guard asks.

Sam lays a calming hand on her shoulder.

Rebecca sighs. "No, officer, I don't have a vender's license. Here." And she hands over both of her shirts.

The officer takes them and frowns. "This is all you've got?"

Sam holds out his empty duffel bag, upside down, and gives it a shake for good measure. "Sorry, officer."

For a few seconds the guard considers taking the two of them in; Rebecca can see it in his face. "All right," he growls. "But if I catch either of you selling any more of this crap today, you're spending the night in jail."

"Yes sir," Sam says.

Rebecca flashes the guard a forced smile.

The guard takes one last long look at the two of them and then cuts between two parked cars into the next aisle over.

"Suck-up!" Rebecca says, jabbing Sam in the ribs.

"It got rid of him, didn't it?"

"I know, I know." They start strolling through the lot again, in the general direction of the stadium. Hardly anyone is vending anymore. "I can't believe how bad it is. They hit us twice in two minutes. I've never seen a scene like this before."

"Me either."

"So," Sam says, clapping his hands together. "I guess you don't have anything to do for the rest of the afternoon either."

Rebecca smiles. "I guess not."

"Walk with me, then?"

"Sure."

The sun is starting to set, which means the show should be starting in a little less than an hour. The evening air blowing in across the river cools them, after an afternoon of summer heat.

They wander into the shadow cast by the stadium, where the lucky ones with tickets are starting to clot up at the gates. The ones looking for tickets swarm anxiously around them, a mob of raised fingers. "Hey, somebody miracle me!" a tall, bushy-haired man nearby, dressed all in orange, is shouting to whoever will listen. "It's my birthday! Don't let me miss seeing the Dead on my birthday!"

The rest of the Deadheads — the ones who have resigned themselves to not getting into the concert at all — gather glumly around their cars, settling in for the long wait for the concert to end. Here and there a few people are still trying to vend, but for the most part the scene is mellowing out. A man in full tie-dye juggles multicolored balls, surrounded by eager-faced children. Sam and Rebecca settle back against the grille of nearby microbus, watching.

Nearby, an old guy in a woven tam, a vest, and Guat pants is showing a tie-dyed T-shirt to a kid in his early teens.

39

Rebecca glances over at him, and catches sight of two uniformed cops — a man and a woman — strolling towards him, between the parked cars.

"Six up!" she shouts out. She takes a few steps towards the old Head. "Six up, brother. Six up!"

The old Head's eyes do a quick sweep of the parking lot around him, but it's already too late. The cops step in right between him and his customer, who slips quietly away. "I thought so," the male cop says to his partner. "Okay, grandpa. I warned you once. Now hand over the bag."

Inside Rebecca, something snaps. "Come on," she orders Sam, and then she marches right into the middle of the whole mess. Sam follows cautiously behind her.

"Come on, sir," the lady cop is saying. "Just give us the merchandise and you're free to go."

"No way," the old Head says, hugging his knapsack to his chest.

"I can't take this anymore!" Rebecca shouts. "What do you have to bug this guy for? He wasn't hurting anybody."

"I don't want to hear it, honey," the male cop tells her. He makes a grab for the knapsack, but the old Deadhead ducks backwards — faster than he looks. "Hand over the bag now," the cop tells him, "or I'm going to take you in."

"He didn't do anything," Rebecca insists, nose-to-nose with the cop now.

A hand clamps on her left arm. "Don't do something you'll regret later," Sam's voice hisses in her ear.

"Don't you guys have any murderers or crack

dealers to catch in this crummy town?" Rebecca asks, struggling in Sam's grip.

"You just watch your mouth," the male cop snaps back at her.

While none of them are looking, the old Deadhead is suddenly gone — tearing off across the parking lot, clutching the knapsack to his chest. The cop curses under his breath and starts after him.

"Let him go!" Rebecca shouts after them. "Bastards! He didn't do anything!"

The lady cop steps forward, fixing a firm hand on Rebecca's right shoulder. "We don't want to have any problems here, do we?" she asks.

"You guys have been after us all day!" Rebecca shouts. "All we want to do is make a little money so we can keep going to the shows. We're not hurting anybody!"

"The band asked us to be here," the cop explains.

"Bullshit!" Rebecca spits. "It was the local government, and you know it."

"It was the band," the cop insists. "They don't want to be held responsible for any illegal activities."

"Illegal activities? It's just a fucking tie-dye!" Rebecca is screaming now, and she shakes her way out of the cop's grip. "Just let him go!"

"Just calm down, lady."

"Rebecca, please!" Sam begs her.

"LET HIM GO, DAMN IT! HE DIDN'T DO ANYTHING!"

"Just move on, lady." the officer orders, making a grab

for Rebecca's free arm.

"LET ME ALONE! LET US BOTH ALONE!"

All this time, the old Head has been leading the other cop on a chase around the edges of the parking lot. He's running well, holding his own against a man half his age, even with the extra weight of the bag of shirts. They've come almost full circle now, heading back to where the chase started. They're both starting to look a little worn out.

"This isn't any of your business," the lady cop is saying. "Now move along before I decide to frisk you."

The old Head whips past them now, the cop just ten feet behind him.

Rebecca twists herself out of Sam's hands and barrels between the two of them.

In the next instant, she and the male cop are sprawled together on the sidewalk, and the old Deadhead has disappeared into the crowd.

"Okay, that's it, you little bitch," the cop growls. "You're going to jail."

"The hell I am," Rebecca says. She scrambles to her feet and starts running.

"I've got her," the lady cop shouts out to her partner, and Rebecca hears a set of footsteps pounding the pavement behind her.

For sixty seconds that seem to last forever, Rebecca sprints around the perimeter of the parking lot, dodging around cars and ducking through clots of Deadheads. But the cop is in as good shape as she is, and Rebecca can't shake her.

Panting, her muscles like tightening bands around her chest, Rebecca steers back past the spot where the chase first started. It's empty now. Sam and the male cop are gone.

Damn, she thinks. I hope I didn't get Sam into any trouble.

"Somebody stop her!" she hears the lady cop shout from behind her, and she picks up her speed.

She zig-zags across the parking lot now, heading in the general direction of the stadium. She makes a sudden left turn, ducking into a knot of a few hundred Deadheads gathered along the path leading to the stadium gate.

One second she has a clear path through the fringes at the edge of the crowd. The next second there's a man standing in her way. Rebecca never even sees him coming.

It's Sam. He grabs her by the sleeve. "Just act casual," he tells her in a low, even voice. "Pretend that we're talking."

"But the cops —"

"Are still following you," he tells her, his eye glinting knowingly. "But they're looking for someone who's running."

"So, how about those Mets?" Rebecca asks, leaning back casually on one foot, pressing her hand down over her aching lungs.

"I think they'll have a pretty good season if they can keep up their pitching," Sam answers easily.

The cop reaches the edge of the crowd and stops just a

few yards away from where Rebecca and Sam are standing. She doesn't look all that worn out, considering she just chased Rebecca, at top speed, twice around the parking lot.

"You're really light on your feet," Sam notes.

"I lettered in track in high school," I tell him. "Cross-country and the four-forty."

"I can tell."

The officer cranes her neck, stretching up over the crowd, searching the faces.

"Don't look at her," Sam says. "She's looking for anybody who's watching her. If you look at her, she'll see you."

"You know a lot about getting rid of cops."

"Let's just say I've had a lot of practice at it."

"I'm sure your parents are very proud of you."

Sam gives her an unreadable smile.

Out of the corner of her eye, Rebecca sees the officer frown a little, skim the faces in the crowd one last time, and then turn away.

"That was amazing!" Rebecca calls out, the relief and surprise spilling out of her. "Why didn't she spot me?"

"Because we all look alike to them," Sam answers. "All she probably remembered about you was that you had long, dark hair and you were wearing a skirt and a tie-dye. That's what half of the women here look like. As soon as you stopped running, as soon as you stopped acting like a target, she couldn't spot you in the crowd."

"That's so wild!"

"What you did was really stupid, you know," Sam tells her. "If she'd been just a little faster, you'd be in handcuffs by now."

"I know, I know," Rebecca says with a shrug. "I didn't even decide to do it. I just did it."

"It was also pretty cool."

Rebecca grabs either side of her skirt and gives a little curtsy. "Cool but stupid. That's me."

"You've got guts," Sam continues. "I really admire that. But if you're going to keep doing shit like that, you're going to need me around to get you out of the trouble you keep getting yourself into."

Rebecca smiles, glancing down at her shoes. "I guess so."

"Listen," Sam says, "the show's about to start. I bet we can find some place in the lots somewhere where we can get pretty good sound."

"Sounds like fun," Rebecca says. "But first, I've got some pot back in my car. Walk with me?"

"I'd love to."

Sam slips his hand into hers, and they walk back across the lots, together through the thinning crowd.

THE LOST GIRL

Marie finishes rolling the joint as Allison pulls off the highway, right into the heart of downtown. "Where's the concert hall?" Allison asks.

Jane, in the front passenger seat, checks the map. "Turn left on Broadway."

"Here?"

"Yeah, here." Allison makes a sharp turn, switching lanes in the process, cutting off a businessman in a Cadillac. He leans on his horn in protest.

"Smooth move," Marie says, blowing gently on the joint to dry the glue.

"You wanna drive?"

"There," Jane says, pointing out her window. "The concert's about a block that way."

"How soon 'til the show?"

Jane checks her watch. "A little over an hour."

"Cool," Allison says. "We made some wicked time."

"But of course," Marie says, leaning forward from the back seat and holding out the joint for the others' inspection. "Wanna toke this baby up?"

"Let's wait until we've found a place to park," Jane says.

"How 'bout there?" Marie asks, pointing. The lot is tiny — enough room for a hundred cars at the most. But it's only half-full, and, from the look of the crowd, they're all going to the show.

Allison makes a sharp left, across traffic and without signaling, and screeches the car to a stop right next to the attendant — an old black man in ragged overalls. "Five bucks," he tells them, completely unfazed by Allison's driving. The three friends haggle and hedge over who'll pay the parking fee, finally coming up with five crumpled ones between them. Allison takes a ticket from the attendant and peals out across the parking lot in one fluid motion.

"Christ, girl," Marie says, as they swerve into an empty space. "We're here, okay? We're not in a hurry anymore."

"I'm sick of driving," Allison returns. "Let's go walking and smoke that nail."

The three friends step out of the car. The sky is just getting dark, and the spring evening is cool and breezy. Their half of the lot is empty, but across the way — the end of the lot closest to the concert hall — a couple hundred Heads have gathered, to kill the time together before the show starts. Even across the lot, the three women can smell the incense in the air, and hear the rhythms of drums.

"Fire?" Marie asks. Jane hands her a lighter.

"Duck down," Jane snaps, as Marie makes to light up then and there. "Jesus. We're right in the middle of downtown."

"People smoking pot at a Phish show?" Allison gasps.

"Who would have thought?"

"It's still illegal."

"Fine," Marie says. The three of them squat down between their car and the rusted red Ford Fairmont that's pulled up next to them. Marie lights the joint, takes a long hit, and hands it to Allison.

Allison has taken her hit, and is passing the joint on to Jane, when the driver's door to the Fairmont swings open. A tall, scruffy boy gets out, hitches up his pants, and plows right through the middle of the three friends without even noticing them.

"Pardon us, asshole!" Allison calls after him.

"Forget it, Al," Marie tells her, taking the joint from Jane. "Just another zomboid."

"Besides," Jane says, "we're here to celebrate." She grins over at Marie, and the two friends exchange a high-five. "Five shows in a week. We actually did it! And it's been the best time of my life!"

"It's been a week to remember," Marie agrees, the words spilling out of her in a cloud of smoke. "It's hard to believe we've all got classes bright and early Monday morning."

"Maybe we do," Allison says. "Maybe we don't." And she jerks her eyebrows up suggestively.

"What are you saying?" Marie asks. "You wanna ditch?"

Allison offers Jane the joint. "You saying you don't want to?"

"Oh, I didn't say that," Marie assures her.

"You guys can't be serious," Jane chimes in, and then

48

she sucks in a lungful of smoke. Only then does she notice a face watching her, peering out the back window of the Fairmont. She nudges Marie. "Hey guys."

They all turn to look at the face now — a girl, maybe a few years younger than the three friends. Jane smiles at her, and the young woman smiles back.

"Looks like some sort of space case."

Jane waves for the girl to join them. The girl pushes the car door open slowly and, in a trance, squats down next to them on the asphalt, hugging her knees.

"Hi."

"Hi."

"My name's Jane. This is Marie, and this madwoman over here is Allison."

"Cool. Where you guys from?"

"We all go to school together. Purdue."

"Spring break," Jane adds.

"You guys are in college?" the girl asks, her left hand absently coiling up inside a lock of her long, straight hair.

"Are you still in high school?"

The girl smiles. "I still should be, I guess."

"You from around here?" Marie asks.

"No," she answers. The others wait for a few seconds, expecting more. "Not really," she adds, to fill the silence.

"I was just wondering if you knew where any cheap motels were around here."

"Want a toke?" Allison asks, holding out the joint.

Again it takes the girl a few seconds to react, like she's

49

on time-delay. "Sure." She takes the joint from Allison and draws in a long, expert hit.

"So what were you sitting in the car for?" Allison wants to know. "It's a gorgeous night out, and you were wasting it in the back seat."

"Oh," the woman says, passing Jane the joint and staring down at her feet. "Well, Brian — my guy — he went out to see if he could score some pot. Told me to wait here for him."

"Cool," Marie says, with a chuckle. "He leaves you behind while he goes to look for drugs, and the drugs come and find you."

"That's poetic justice for you," Allison agrees.

Jane's hit all but finishes the joint. She pulls her roach clip out of her hair, fastens it to the smoldering butt, and passes it on to Marie. "I don't think there's more than a hit or two left," she announces.

They finish the joint in silence, Allison getting the last hit (little more than a smoldering wad of greasy paper by that point) and dropping the remains into the gravel at their feet. "Well," she announces, "we've gotta go. Been nice."

"Yeah, see ya."

"Nice to meet you," Jane says, giving the girl a quick hug. "And you shouldn't let your boyfriend boss you around like that."

"There goes Jane," Marie murmurs to Allison, just loud enough for Jane to hear. "Still trying to liberate the world." Jane smiles and blows Marie a kiss.

"Come on," Allison orders, and she makes a bee-line across the lot. Jane and Marie trot after her.

"So what's your rush?" Jane asks.

"We need to get to the gates now if we want seats up front."

"No way," Jane says. "Not up front. Not again."

"'Not again?'" Allison mimics. "What do you mean? It's the best."

"The best?" Jane counters. "Getting crushed in by the crowd all night? Not even having room enough to dance?"

"Sounds great to me," Allison tells her. "Listen, you can sit in the nose-bleeds if you want to. We'll meet you back at the car after the show."

"Marie?"

"Come on, Jane," Marie pleads. "It is our last show."

"Well I'm sure as hell not going to sit by myself," Jane says, and she jogs to catch up to the other two.

"That's another thing," Allison says, as she leads them across the street — against the light — and into the first trickles of concert-goers heading to the hall. "Who says it needs to be our last show? I mean really."

"You're serious."

"Dead serious."

"Allison —" Jane begins.

"Why do we have to stop now?" Allison asks them. "There's only a week left of tour — four more shows. We just ditch a week's worth of classes. Hell, I'd work my ass of for the rest of the semester just to go to four more shows."

51

"We can't afford it."

"We can if we sleep in the car. Be imaginative."

"What would our folks say?" Marie asks.

"Who says they have to know?" Allison tells her. "Think about it. We all call in tomorrow saying that we got back safely, and no one will be the wiser."

"That's fine with me," Marie says. "And I know your folks don't give a damn. But what about Jane?"

They reach the front doors of the concert hall. A small crowd, mostly men, has gathered, waiting for the doors to open so they can be the first ones into the hall.

"God, I love general admission," Allison says. "What time is it?"

"Six-fifteen."

"Hmn. Gates probably open at six-thirty." She starts worming her way through the crowd. "Come on, guys."

Marie shakes her head. "The chick never stops, does she?"

"Nope," Jane answers, "but she'll get us right up to the front."

"Gotta love her," Marie says, and the two of them follow in the wake Allison is cutting through the crowd.

After ten minutes of creative maneuvers, taking advantage of her sex appeal with most of the crowd and her six feet of height with everyone else, Allison gets them to within two feet of the door. "This is cool," she announces, when she finally feels that she's gone far enough. "We may not be in the first row, but second row's just as good."

"About doing the rest of tour . . . " Jane prompts.

"Yeah," Marie says. "You know how Jane's dad is. I was shocked enough that he let her tour at all."

"You worry too much," Allison tells them. "We can handle it. Do you want to tour for another week or don't you?"

"Well, sure, yeah, I guess," Jane says.

"Then fuck it. Just do it. Okay?"

Jane smiles. "Okay." She holds up her left hand, and Allison clasps it in her right.

"Okay?" Allison asks Marie.

"Okay!" Marie echoes, and she takes up each of her friends' free hands. "Let's do it!"

"What do you think?" Jane asks. "Is the world ready for us?"

"If they aren't," Allison says with a wicked smile, "then they damn well better get ready." The three friends drop hands, and Allison gives Jane a light cuff on the shoulder.

"What is it with your dad anyway?" she asks. "I mean, it's not like you're not eighteen or anything."

Jane shakes her head. "I guess it's just that, ever since Mom died, I'm sort of all he's got."

"He needs a new hobby then, girl," Marie tells her. "Stamp collecting. Anything. You've got to get him out of your life."

"I'm trying, I'm trying," Jane assures her.

"What time is it?" Allison asks.

Jane checks her watch again. "Almost half-past."

"Come on," Allison shouts to the closed doors. "It's time, man. Let us in."

"Not for a while yet," the guy standing next to her says.

Allison looks him up and down for a few seconds, as if she's trying to decide whether he's worth her notice or not. "What's that supposed to mean?"

"Didn't you hear? It's been all over the radio."

"What?"

"They're only going to be letting people in one at a time," he answers. "There's some girl who ran away from home to follow the band. So her folks flew into town this afternoon. They're going to be right at the gate, checking everybody out as they go into the show."

"If that's the case," Allison says, leaning back on one foot and stretching up to her full height — a good six inches above his, "they should be letting us in sooner, not later. It could take hours for Mom and Pop to scope everybody out."

"Don't ask me," the guy says, trying hard not to look like he's retreating. "I just heard the news. I don't know anything else about it." And with that, he turns back to his friends.

"Creep," Allison mumbles to Jane and Marie.

"Can you believe that?" Marie says. "How humiliating. To have your folks come all the way out here just to drag your ass home?"

"I can imagine it," Jane says. "Sounds like something my dad would do."

Allison shakes her head.

"Holy shit!" Marie shouts out suddenly.

"What?"

"That chick! The one in the car next to ours."

"What about her?"

"Do you think she could be the lost girl?"

Jane nods. "She did look a little uncomfortable when we asked her where she was from."

"Yeah," Marie says. "And she never did tell us what her name was."

"Well, if that was the lost girl, I have no idea why Mummy and Daddy are so hot to get her back," Allison announces with a sneer. "She wasn't exactly a prize."

"That just makes it worse," Marie says. "Come on, you were sixteen once. What if she ran off with that zomboid boyfriend of hers and he's a real jerk or something?"

"Well, if it was her they were looking for," Allison says, "her folks'll spot her trying to get into the show."

"If she's going to the show tonight."

"You worry too much, Marie. If the kid took it on herself to run away, she can sure as hell take care of herself."

"I hope so," Jane says.

That ends that conversation. They all turn and stare at the doors.

"Let's do a doobie," Marie chirps.

"Not here," Jane says.

"Yeah," Allison agrees. "Can't it wait 'til we get inside, you dope-head?"

Marie shrugs and does a little dance. "I know what I like."

"Yeah, I guess —"

But Allison's comment — all conversations altogether — come to a sudden stop at the sound of chains rattling from the other side of the door. Then there is an echoing thud, and a single door, right in front of where the three friends are standing, swings open.

Like a single creature, the crowd surges forward. The friends don't walk through the doors so much as ride the tide in.

Jane keeps an eye out as they shuffle through a bottle-neck, past a ticket window with the shades pulled up. Inside, a pair of security guards, a police officer, and a worried-looking middle-aged man watch as the crowd trickles past them. Another two officers are waiting at the far end of the bottleneck, ears to their walkie-talkies.

For an instant, Jane and the man exchange glances. He seems ordinary enough — just another hard-working family man. She can read volumes in his eyes. There is concern for his missing daughter, of course, right there on the surface. There is a lot of doubt too — of his ability as a father, of his reasons for being there. But under all that, what she reads is amazement. He's led such a sheltered life — living in the same small town he was born in, working the same job for thirty years. He's never once imagined that the same world he lives in can also conjure up such people as those flowing past him now: acid heads, freaks, flower children, spinners, madmen. This is more of the world than he has ever wanted to see, more than he has

56

ever wanted his daughter to see. Shocked and sickened as he is, though, love and worry for his daughter keep him there, watching for something familiar in that river of madness.

That same river carries Jane through the bottleneck, past the two officers with the walkie-talkies and out into the open lobby. With a whoop, Allison races for the auditorium doors, and Jane and Marie do their best to keep up with her.

Am I so different, Jane asks herself, have I changed so much, that my own father looked me right in the eye and didn't even recognize me?

She doesn't know. And she wonders for the longest time, long into the first set of the concert, whether it bothers her or not.

RAIN SHOW

They arrive at RFK Stadium at three o'clock in the afternoon. The scene is already in full swing. John, Elizabeth, and Danny divide the last seventy of the T-shirts between them. Zeke, the hitchhiker they picked up at the Raleigh show two days before, stands off to one side, looking bored.

"With three of us selling and eight more shows, we could each sell three a day and still sell out," Elizabeth tells Danny and John. "In other words, sell as hard as you like, but there's really no hurry."

John nods.

"Cool," Danny says. "I could use an easy day."

"Enjoy yourself," Elizabeth urges him.

"I intend to," Danny tells her, his mind swimming with thoughts of the secret that Zeke had shared with him the night before: an eight-ounce medicine bottle filled to the top with pure high-grade liquid LSD. "Straight from the lab," Zeke had bragged, grinning widely.

But when Danny turns to go, Zeke has already disappeared. As tall as Zeke is, though, it's easy enough to find him again; craning his neck, Danny catches sight of him striding away through the crowd. Swinging his backpack of T-shirts over one shoulder, Danny runs to catch up. He trots along after Zeke, always one pace behind him.

"Hey, man. Do you mind if I hang out with you today?"

"No," Zeke says.

"What are you gonna do all day?"

"Deal."

"The liquid?" Danny asks, almost too loudly.

"No," Zeke answers. "That's for my own private use. I have some paper too."

"Cool," Danny says. "I was selling paper for the first part of tour. It's been selling really well, too, 'cause everybody's jonesing so much for weed."

Zeke nods.

They come to a tunnel under the main highway, and pass through it to the next parking lot over. At one end of this lot, across a four-lane road, is the stadium itself. At the other end is a strip of grass, a line of trees, and then the Anacosta River.

Zeke pauses for a second, hands on his hips, and runs his eyes over the aisles of parked cars. Then he glances over at Danny. "Aren't you going to start selling?"

Danny shrugs. "I don't really feel like it. Besides, you heard what Elizabeth said. There's no rush."

"Rush nothing," Zeke tells him. "I heard that there are going to be undercover cops all over the lots today. That's why I need you to vend. I figure that anybody who stops to look at your shirt is going to be a real Head, and it'll be safe for me to sell to them. The cops'll be the ones who are too busy sniffing around for drugs to bother looking at a T-shirt. What do you say?"

"Sure. I guess so," Danny says. He thinks about Zeke's bottle of liquid, and licks his lips. "Why the hell not?"

It works out just the way Zeke predicted. Four out of every five of Danny's customers show at least a mild interest when Zeke comes up and starts his own sales pitch. And some of Zeke's customers are in a good enough mood to buy one of Danny's shirts as well. By five o'clock, Danny has sold fifteen T-shirts. Zeke has sold over a hundred hits of acid, five and ten hits at a time.

Meanwhile, as the afternoon wears on, the clouds push down lower and lower in the sky, and the air becomes more wet and heavy. "It's gonna rain," Danny notes.

Zeke grabs Danny by the collar. "Look," he says. Just ten feet from them, a uniformed police officer marches up to a kid loitering by a car and flashes his badge. The kid turns to run, but the officer already has a firm grip on his arm. Two seconds later, the kid is face-down on the asphalt, and the officer is on top of him, fastening on a pair of handcuffs.

"What the hell was that about?" Danny asks.

"Shh," Zeke hisses. "Look over there."

Again Danny follows Zeke's eyes. A hundred yards further down the aisle, another uniformed officer approaches yet another kid. This one doesn't even try to run. He turns around and assumes the position against the side of a van.

"He's probably clean by now," Zeke says. "But it won't make any difference."

"What's going on?"

"Follow me," Zeke orders, and he charges further down the aisle.

They end up witnessing a whole string of arrests. In each case, the officer comes up to the unsuspecting person without warning, as if the police were just picking people at random.

"What is it, Zeke?"

"Drug busts," Zeke explains. "A classic set-up. They have one undercover cop buy drugs from as many different dealers as he can. Then, maybe hours later, the cops just go around and clean house. Simple, efficient, and effective. It'll look great in the morning papers. The worst part of it is, you never know which of your customers was the cop — at least not until the trial."

"That shits, man." Danny says.

Zeke shrugs. "They're just doing their jobs. Besides, dealing wouldn't be any fun if there weren't any cops to duck."

"Hey," Danny calls out suddenly, grabbing Zeke by the tail of his Guat shirt. "How do you know that you didn't sell to an undercover today? How do you know they aren't coming for you next?"

"I don't."

And Zeke walks on, calmly, his hands laced behind his

61

back. Danny stands frozen in place for a moment, peering through the crowd around him for the approaching officer. Then he finds his legs again and rushes to catch up.

"Maybe we should lay low for a while," Danny suggests, breathless.

"Why? If they've got me, they've got me."

"I don't know," Danny says. "I just don't like cops."

"You're not supposed to."

"You're almost sold out anyway, and I don't feel like selling anymore."

Zeke sighs. "Okay, Danny. We can stop for a while. But you really shouldn't let the cops rule your life like this." He taps Danny on the chest with the back of his hand. "Come on. I thought I heard a whippet tank."

"Whippets?"

"Let's go," Zeke suggests. "I'll buy you one."

"Sure thing."

They find the nitrous dealer easily, by following the hissing sound that occasionally rises above the general noises of the crowd. He's selling out of a half-sized metal canister, hidden under a blanket in the trunk of his car. Between each sale, he turns to his waiting customers and begs them to fan out — to not look so much like a line.

"Man, I love this stuff," Danny says as they join the crowd.

He watches hungrily as they inch closer and closer to the canister. But then, suddenly, the line ahead of them starts breaking up. "Sorry," the whippet dealer is saying.

"The Heat's getting to be a little bit too much out here, so we're going to have to close up shop." He shuts his trunk and leans back against it.

"Damn pigs," Danny grumbles, as he and Zeke stroll away.

"How about some of the liquid instead?" Zeke offers.

Danny feels his face break into a wide smile. "Sure. I thought you'd never ask."

They step into the woods together. Zeke carefully lifts the bottle out of his pocket, cupped between his two hands. "How many do you want?"

Danny's eyes smolder. "Four."

"Four?" Zeke asks. He smiles. "Good. You're going to love this."

Danny tilts his head back and closes his eyes. Four drops of the cool, thin liquid hit the back of his throat. He opens his eyes again in time to see Zeke empty half the eye dropper into his own mouth.

"Oh, man," Danny says. "You're gonna fly!"

Zeke smiles again, and raises one eyebrow.

And then, once again, comes the familiar hiss of a whippet tank — this time from about two hundred yards away.

Danny and Zeke exchange glances.

"Do you still want some?" Zeke asks.

"Sure."

They have trouble finding the tank this time, until they realize that the sounds are coming from the woods. They trudge through the underbrush, and find the same dealer that shut down his business just a few minutes before. The nitrous tank is leaning up against a tree now, and the dealer is trying, unsuccessfully, to muffle the hissing sound with a towel. There aren't as many people waiting at the tank now, and after just another minute Danny and Zeke are at the head of the line.

"You moved," Zeke notes to the dealer.

"Had to," the dealer tells them. "They'd just busted another nitrous dealer in the next lot over."

"D.E.A. or locals?"

"Just locals, but that's enough."

"Are they still busting for acid too?"

"Hell, brother," the dealer snaps back. "I don't know. I'm just trying to cover my own ass. How many?"

"Two."

"Ten bucks."

Zeke and the dealer exchange money for balloons. "Don't let anybody see you walking out of the woods with these," the dealer cautions them. "And watch out for low-flying branches. No refunds if you bust 'em yourself."

"Cool," Zeke says.

"Let's do 'em right here, in the woods," Danny suggests, on their way back through the trees.

"Watch this," Zeke says. He puts the nozzle of the balloon to his lips, and in the next second the balloon is empty, and Zeke's lungs are full.

"Jesus," Danny gasps.

The empty balloon drops from Zeke's fingers. He smiles dreamily, his eyes fixed and glazed. Then, suddenly, his skin goes pale, his eyes roll backwards, and his knees give away underneath him. He crumples into a ball on the forest floor.

"Shit!" Danny calls out. He jumps to Zeke's side, almost losing his grip on his own balloon, and checks to make sure Zeke didn't hit his head in the fall. Zeke, meanwhile, is grinning from ear to ear now, and murmuring something to himself.

"Zeke? You okay, man?"

"Wonderful," Zeke mumbles.

Danny shrugs, settles down with his back up against a tree, and tries to empty his entire balloon at once, just like Zeke did. He manages only half of it, but it starts his head spinning so fast and light, and suddenly his hand is empty anyway,

and his whole body is tingling just under the skin, and the skin is numb,

and he closes his eyes and he isn't

there anymore.

Light and

warm.

Empty.

I —

From far away, he hears a voice. It bounces and echoes around inside his skull:

65

"Oh, man. You lost the rest of your balloon!"

Like a scuba diver kicking up from the depths, swimming up towards the light to the real world, Danny slowly forces his head to clear. He finds the ground underneath him. He presses backwards until he can feel the bark of the tree cutting against his back. He listens, and Zeke's voice floats out to him:

"How much of it did you do?"

"A lot," Danny hears himself saying.

"That's good, because you lost the rest of it."

Danny peels his eyes open sleepily, and looks down at his hand. It's empty. Zeke, grinning, points to a small scrap of orange rubber hanging from a branch about twenty feet above them.

"You let go of it when you blacked out, and it flew up there."

Danny grins back. "I don't give a shit. What a rush!"

"Oh, yeah."

"How's your head?" Danny asks. "That was really cool, man. You did the fish. You just passed right fucking out."

"I'm fine," Zeke assures him. "I didn't mean to scare you. Sometimes I black out, and sometimes I don't. But I love nitrous. I mean, acid is really intense and all, but when you're on it, you're still where you are, you know what I mean? Everything looks odd, but you're still here on Earth. But with nitrous, when you take enough of it, you disappear. You're somewhere else."

Danny nods. "Nitrous is the best."

"Come on," Zeke says, pulling out and lighting up a cigarette. "Let's head towards the stadium."

They step back out of the woods, and Zeke strides purposefully in some random direction, with Danny jogging along behind him. They come, finally, to a parking lot on the inland side of the stadium. At the far end, beyond a simple chain-link fence, are the tattered buildings of the D.C. slums.

"Why are Dead shows always in the bad parts of town?" Danny asks.

"I like it," Zeke tells him.

Danny's starting to get that feeling in his stomach now — the same feeling he gets every time he doses. He doesn't feel queasy exactly. It's just a dull pressure, like a fist pressing down from the inside, and there's an odd taste in his mouth.

He and Zeke wander around the lot for another hour. Danny sells three more shirts, and Zeke sells another thirty hits of acid. Already, Danny feels as if he's just floating across the asphalt, and his own voice sounds muffled and far away. By the time Zeke leads him over to the stadium gate, the people passing by on either side are streaming rainbow trails behind them.

In the clot of people waiting to get in, he and Zeke get separated. Danny picks a group of people that passingly resemble a line, and shuffles along in it until he comes to the gate. A guard searches his backpack and then waves him through.

Zeke is waiting for him inside. "There you are."

"Here I am," Danny returns. He can't stop his mouth from grinning.

"Our seats are all the way up in the nosebleed section," Zeke says, checking his stub.

"Hell with that," Danny grunts.

"I agree. Come on."

Danny follows Zeke through the mobbed hallways of the stadium: around the lines at the concession stands, through the clots of people loitering by the bathrooms, up a steep concrete ramp to the mezzanine level. All the while Danny fixes his eyes on the weave of the back of Zeke's Guatemalan shirt. The black and purple stripes buck, melt, and twist every time Zeke takes a step.

Zeke glances back to make sure Danny is still behind him. "Come on," he urges, and then leads Danny up a short ramp and out into open air.

A damp breeze wipes across Danny's face as he steps out into the lower deck of the stands. The stadium is already half full, and the field is a tightly-packed mass of multi-colored shirts and long hair. The taper's section, right behind the sound board, bristles with microphone stands — each with its own little umbrella to protect the equipment if it should start to rain.

"Close enough?" Zeke asks. Danny nods.

The two of them settle into a pair of empty seats. Almost immediately, Zeke elbows Danny in the ribs. "Where's that pot?"

"Oh, sorry. I don't want any, but you can have some. Here." He digs through his pocket. The cloth feels like a cotton mouth sucking on his hand. He finds the pipe and the bag of pot, and hands them to Zeke.

Danny can feel and smell the people pressing in around him. He lights a cigarette, and then blows out a lungful of smoke and watches it twist and dance up into the grey screen of clouds. Then he closes his eyes, and his head lolls backwards. His joints feel loose and open; his arms dangle at his sides. His skin tingles.

"Cool."

His eyes fix on the tie-dye some woman two rows in front of him is wearing. The colors burn and glow, leaving bright after-images. He is lost in the patterns for several minutes.

Danny feels a light throbbing in his fingers. He looks down. The cigarette has burned down almost to his skin. He drops it on the concrete, and the coal spins and burns a red trail after it as it rolls down under the seat in front of him.

"Do you want any more?" comes a voice from behind him.

Danny turns. He watches the world spinning around him, a shimmering blur. Zeke's vague face comes into view. He's holding up the medicine bottle, and smiling.

"No way, man. I'd never come down."

"So never come down," Zeke says.

Zeke's smile glitters in Danny's mind.

"Sure. Why the fuck not?"

Zeke pulls Danny back down into his seat. "Open your mouth." Danny does so. Zeke squeezes out another drop of acid onto Danny's tongue. Danny feels it rolling down his throat, like a bead of mercury. He can hear it sliding down, in the silence.

Zeke smiles, and slowly screws the top back onto the bottle.

Danny is suddenly aware of the crowd again. People are getting restless. The band should have started by now, and, worse yet, the clouds are starting to thicken and boil across the sky.

"Oh, man!" Danny hears himself call out. "It's gonna rain for sure!"

"Hey, look," Zeke calls out, pointing.

Set up above the stage is a make-shift plywood roof, from which the jet black stage lights dangle upside-down like giant bats. There are blue plastic tarps spread over the top of the roof, to keep water away from the lights if it rains. As strong as the wind is down in the stands, it's even stronger at the top of the stadium. The corner of one of the tarps has ripped free. It flaps wildly in the breeze, like a blue flame. It dances along the edge of the rooftop; you can hear it snapping in the wind all the way at the other end of the stadium.

Danny's hands tug and coil one of the straps of his backpack.

"Do you see them?" Zeke asks, pointing again.

Danny follows Zeke's finger. Two roadies have crawled

out onto the roof. They creep down the gentle slope to the very edge, trying desperately to catch hold of the loose tarp.

In the wind, at the edge of the roof, a hundred feet above the stage.

Danny closes his eyes.

He can see one of the roadies make a wild grab at the tarp. He totters forward. The tarp picks up the wind like a sail, flinging him off the roof, like a child tossing away a toy. He falls, his arms and legs struggling against the open air. He can hear the wind rushing past his ears, he can feel the sudden jarring stillness as his body slams into the stage below.

Danny opens his eyes.

The roadies have managed to smooth out the tarp against the roof, and are tying it tightly back into place.

"Wow. Fuck. Cool."

As soon as the roadies have crawled back off the roof, the Grateful Dead takes the stage. The crowd roars — a single, swarming, monstrous beast.

The concert is a liquid succession of music and lyrics. They start with a sweet and easy "Let the Good Times Roll." Danny rocks back and forth to the rhythm of the song, singing the words softly to himself. The band then eases into a cool version of "Feel Like a Stranger." The notes press in around Danny, cradling him, tossing him up into the air, flinging him down. He closes his eyes, and lets the music carry him where it will.

He is lost in the patterns of color swirling just under his

eyelids. The top of his skull separates from his body like a hat. He can feel the wind tracing patterns across the surface of his brain. Even the concrete under his feet is lost to him. He drifts in a universe all his own, where only colors and music exist. Even Danny himself is not there. Only colors and the music, and a scrap of lyrics now and then.

He fumbles across his thigh until his fingers find the bulge of his crumpled cigarette pack. He finds a cigarette, and his lighter, and pulls a lungful of smoke into the liquid universe around him. The smoke is liquid, too, swimming through the music like a ghost, staining everything in grey.

"Hey," calls a voice from somewhere. "Did you just feel a raindrop?"

If his father could just try this once: to feel the colors sliding across his skin, to see the music dancing around him, pressing against him like a wild lover, cutting into him like a gentle razor. If his mother could just once feel the acid seeping through her body like a blinding light. If she could just feel her heart jumping double time, feel each and every drop of her blood pushing through the tiniest veins, feel each of the hairs all over her body tugging at her skin. Feel her arms and legs dangling free as she floats away from the earth.

Something brushes up against Danny's arm far below him, back down in the jumble of Washington, D.C. Danny nudges back down through the clouds to see what's going on. He opens his eyes. The crowd spreads out around him like a fiery blanket. Everyone twists and jumps and struggles

72

against one another, lost to the music.

Danny finds himself looking down into a face, split open with a bright red grin. It's Zeke, his head wide and flat like a cartoon. Zeke smiles and holds the medicine dropper up to Danny's mouth. He squeezes a drop against Danny's lips. It trickles, a melting pebble of ice, down Danny's chin, and under his shirt, across his chest, until it seeps into his skin and is gone.

Stuck back in his body now, Danny screws shut his eyes. He feels the music snaking into him. It flows into his muscles, and his arms lift up and start weaving around one another. His head bows forward and back again. His feet shuffle in slow, matching circles. He loses his balance, and stumbles back. Something catches him.

He's sitting down now. His arms coil and strike to the beat of the music. His head snaps like a tarp flying loose in the wind.

His hands pull across his face, and they are wet. He holds his head in his hands, his body still thrusting to the beat. The crowd starts to scream as one single, horrible creature. It is a battle cry. He hears the stomping of feet.

He closes his eyes again. Disconnected images flash across the dark screen of him mind. He wonders what Stacie is doing now, and for a second he can almost feel her.

Danny, the set is over.

Danny, the set is over.

Danny —

It is Zeke's voice. "Danny, the set is over."

Danny opens his eyes.

"Hey, man," comes Zeke's voice from beside him. "Are you still with us, man?"

"No."

"That's cool," Zeke says. "I just wanted to tell you that you were still dancing, and the set's been over for a couple minutes now."

Danny turns his empty face up into the sky; it fills with water like a bowl.

"Hey, man. It's raining."

"It's pouring," Zeke tells him. "It started halfway through the set. Where were you, I wonder?"

Danny looks down at the stadium field. Most of the Heads are still there, standing out in the open, letting the rain drench them. They dance and splash and kick through the water gathering in pools in the grass.

"Let's go down to the field!" Danny cries out.

"Okay."

Zeke leads him down to the bottom of the stands. There isn't a guard anywhere to be seen, and they wander casually down onto the field. The rain is spilling down now, streaming out of the sky. Danny's clothes and hair cling to him, pasted to his skin with rainwater. All around them, people are shouting and laughing, splashing one another, sliding back and forth through the deep patches of fresh mud.

"Hey, Danny!"

And Zeke's body slams against him, throwing him into

a lake-sized puddle.

The mud is cold and alive. Its fingers grip at his hands as Danny struggles to stand up. "Hey, man," he says, and he starts stamping his feet, splashing beads of water and balls of mud all around him. Someone pushes another Head into the puddle, and he and Danny start circling, throwing clumps of mud at one another. A gust of wind bursts across the field, driving nails of rain into Danny's skin. He slips and lands flat on his back. He sinks down into the water.

Danny opens his eyes up into the rain. Zeke, hovering over him, reaches a pale, flat hand down towards Danny's face.

He's going to push me under. He's going to drown me.

Zeke grabs the front of Danny's shirt, and pulls him to his feet in one easy motion. "Look at you, man," Zeke says.

Danny spits a mouthful of mud out at Zeke's feet. "Jesus, I love rain shows."

"As long as you're enjoying yourself."

Danny smiles back dreamily.

"Want to go see if we can work our way up to the front?"

"Cool."

Zeke nods, and starts pushing his way forward through the crowd. Danny follows mindlessly. His sandals are heavy with water and mud. All around them are Deadheads dancing wildly, as if the sound of the rainfall itself were beautiful music. Thunder explodes directly overhead, and the crowd answers with a unanimous cheer.

Then, right in the thick of the storm, the Grateful Dead

comes back out onto the stage. The Deadheads out in the field, still dancing, still splashing around handfuls of water and mud, raise their voices into a cheer that drowns out even the thunder itself. After exchanging a few random notes, the band drifts into a soft, easy melody.

"'Box of Rain,'" a few Deadheads nearby call out.

"'Box of Rain,'" Danny hears himself saying. "What a trip!" And he leans his head back so that the raindrops beat into his face, and he starts to laugh.

Danny gives Zeke a playful shove on the arm. Zeke slugs him back; Danny's shoulder burns and stings, but he's still not deep enough into his body to really feel it.

"Jesus," Danny says, combing the rainwater back across his scalp with one hand. "Jesus, I love the rain."

BAD TRIP

"There you are!" comes a voice from behind her. Jenny puts down the crystal earrings she'd been thinking of buying and spins around.

Dee pushes her way from out of the general motion of the crowd. "Jeez, Jenny! I've been looking all over for you! Brad and Andy are ready to go in!"

Jenny checks her watch. "The show doesn't start for an hour yet."

Dee shrugs. "They want to go in early."

"What the hell for?"

"Hell if I know," Dee answers. "Ask your boyfriend. He's the one who's got the stick up his ass."

Jenny sighs. "Where are they?"

"Follow me."

The scene is just reaching its peak for the day. As Jenny and Dee fight their way down the center aisle of the parking lot, the cries from hawkers rise up all around them. Every fifteen feet or so they have to navigate around yet another clog in the flow of traffic — a beer vender, a group of security guards, a car fighting to inch its way through the crowd.

"Asshole," Dee grumbles in Jenny's ear. "Probably just

trying to get a better parking space."

They join the press of people at the overpass, climb across, and come out by one of the main gates of the stadium. Brad and Andy are there waiting, standing off to one side. Andy is pulling anxiously on a cigarette. Brad taps his foot and bobs his head to some song that only he can hear.

"It's about time," Andy snaps, as Jenny and Dee come up to meet them. "Let's get going."

"What do you want to go in so early for?" Jenny asks Brad.

"I just want to go in early is all," Brad answers. He holds out his hand. "Here."

Sitting in the center of Brad's palm are two hits of acid.

"Oh, I don't know, Brad," Jenny says. "I don't know if my head's in the right place."

"We all dropped, Jenny," Andy tells her, flicking his cigarette butt into the grass.

Jenny glances over at Dee, who nods.

"You don't want to be the only one, do you, Jen?" Brad asks.

Jenny sighs. "Well, I sure as hell don't want to be stuck nursemaiding the three of you all the way home." She takes the small scrap of paper out of Brad's hand.

"Get it, girl!" Dee says.

"Just don't lose me tonight, woman," Jenny returns, and she slips the paper into her mouth. It is only the third time in her life that she's taken LSD, and the first time that she's taken more than one hit.

"Are we ready, then?" Brad asks. Without waiting for an answer, he strides over to the gate. The others follow after him

Even this long before the show is supposed to start, there's already a mob of people waiting to get into the stadium. Jenny gets separated from each of her friends, one by one, in the crowd. Brad and Andy keep pressing forward, anxious and impatient, until Jenny and Dee finally lose sight of them. Then, as they come up to the security checkpoint, the guards wave Dee by, but stop Jenny to frisk her and give her fanny-pack a careful search. When they finally let her through, there isn't a familiar face in sight. It takes her a panicked minute to find her three friends — huddled together off to one side of a concession stand. Andy frowns up at her, and Brad checks his watch. It's forty-five minutes to the show now, and the stadium is starting to fill up. Excited voices echo in the concrete hallways.

"So, where to?" Dee asks.

"Our seats are shit," Brad answers immediately. "Let's go up front."

And now Jenny knows why Brad wanted to get into the stadium as early as possible. "No way."

"Oh, c'mon, Jen. Why not?"

"We've had this discussion before," Jenny tells him. "It's too loud, and it's too crowded. You've got people cramming all around you all night. You can't even sit down during the set break."

"But you're right there, man," Andy chimes in. "It's the best."

"No way," Jenny insists.

"Yeah, c'mon guys," Dee says. "Let's just go sit somewhere up in the stands."

Brad shakes his head. "Not the stands, man. That sucks."

"Okay, let me put it this way," Jenny tells him. "I'm not about to tell you what to do. You can sit anywhere you want. You can go down front if you want to. But Dee and I are going to get some seats up in the stands."

"It's really cool in the stands, guys," Dee says. "If we sit on the lake side of the stadium, we'll be able to see the Sears Tower."

"I can see the Sears Tower any time I want to," Andy returns.

"Nah, man," Brad cuts in, silencing his friend with a pat on the shoulder. "The ladies are right. Let's just stretch out up in the stands and relax for the evening."

Andy still looks a little sour about it, but he agrees.

"Cool," Jenny says. "Are we all settled then?"

"Sure," Brad says. "Let me and Andy get a couple brews, and we can go find some place to sit."

"Cool."

"You two wait right here," Brad says. Jenny thinks for a second that there's something funny about the look on his face, but then she realizes that it's just the acid — warm in her belly, and just starting to seep into her brain — playing tricks on her.

With a grin and a wave, Brad and Andy disappear in the crowd.

Jenny and Dee stand with their backs up against one of the support columns nearby. Deadheads stream all around them now, weaving in and around one another in a shapeless dance. The hallway is a river of flowing tie-dye. Here and there, stray Deadheads gather in eddies and backwashes along the concrete walls. Everyone's excited about the show. The sounds of their voices echo and mix into a solid mass of sound.

"Some scene today, huh?" Jenny asks.

"Yeah. It was pretty cool," Dee returns. "I did a whole mess of balloons."

Jenny shakes her head. "You shouldn't do so much of that stuff, you know. It's bad for the ozone."

Dee shrugs.

"How many hits did you take?"

"Three."

"Three?"

"That's nothing," Dee tells her. "Brad and Andy took six each."

"Six? You're joking!"

Dee sighs, and shakes her head again. "Nope. They dared each other to do it."

"We'll never get them home."

"I know, I know," Dee agrees. "But how was I going to stop them?"

"I'm getting really sick of this shit," Jenny says. "All

81

those two think about is themselves. And they're getting worse. Every time I try to talk to Brad about it he just tells me that I'm cramping his style."

"Andy always tells me that he doesn't need another mother."

"Yeah, that's all good and fine when they're <u>dropping</u> the acid," Jenny complains. "But who's going to have to take care of them when they're tripping so hard they don't even know their own names?"

Dee grunts noncommittally, and they fall back into silence, watching the motions of the crowd around them.

Jenny can definitely feel the acid working on her now. There's an oily coating in the back of her throat, and her skin is crawling with ants. She spends ten whole minutes with her eyes closed, running her hands through her hair, feeling the soft electricity flowing down her fingers. Maybe she was wrong about where her head was at for this trip. Maybe a good dosing is exactly what she needed.

With her eyes closed, and her ears swimming with the undecipherable clamor of echoing voices, it feels to Jenny suddenly as if she is all alone. She is floating safe in her own dark universe. Even the column underneath her, pressed up against her back, isn't real. She can just lie there, and not think of anything. She is safe and alone.

Then a hand grabs her arm.

Jenny lets out a shriek. Her eyes fly open. The world spins around her as she finds herself suddenly on her feet.

"Jesus, Jen."

"Sorry," Jenny says.

"What time is it?"

Jenny checks her watch. "The show starts in ten minutes."

"Damn," Dee growls. "Where did those two jokers go?"

The idea comes to both women at once. They glance back at one another.

"You don't think —?" Dee asks.

"They damn well better not have," Jenny says.

"What do we do?"

Jenny finds herself staring into Dee's eyes, marveling at the way the pupils have swelled up into deep black pools. It changes the way her entire face looks: more innocent, more ethereal, like an elfin child.

"Maybe the beer lines were really long," Dee suggests.

Jenny nods. "One of us should stay here, and the other one should go looking for them."

"I'll go," Dee volunteers. "I need to pee anyway. Don't go anywhere."

"Don't forget about me."

"Cool." And then Dee, too, disappears into the crowd.

Goddamn son of a bitch bastard. Gets six hits into him and just wanders off and does whatever he damn well pleases. Forgets the hell about me. But when this is all over — tomorrow morning or tomorrow night or whenever he ends up coming down — he's going to say that I was the one being an asshole. Damn. I need to end this. He doesn't give a shit about me. All he thinks about is himself.

83

But then, as the heat of this first rage starts to fade, a flood of memories comes to her. The first day they met, at a show two summers ago, out in the lots after the concert. The day they borrowed her brother's motorcycle and rode out to the Indiana Dunes. The first night they kissed. The first night they made love.

The first night they fought.

Then, from all around her, vibrating up through the concrete all around her, comes the distorted sounds of over-amplified music. The noises are barely recognizable as a tune, and God only knows what song it is.

"Great," Jenny grumbles to herself. "I'm left here all alone, and I can't even enjoy the show."

Even though the concert has started, the hallway is still swimming with Heads: rushing to their seats, rushing to the bathroom, rushing to the concession stands, spinning wildly right in the middle of the flow of traffic, smoking pot away in the far corners. But even with this wild parade streaming all around her (leaving rainbow trails as they go), Jenny feels all the more alone.

And then Jenny realizes that people are staring at her as they move past her. Each face that floats past fixes on her for just an instant. Brows furrow. Eyes narrow. Lips frown.

Jenny wipes a hand across her mouth, then under her nose, then through her hair. She checks to make sure that her clothes are all on straight.

Her eyes settle on a tall Head in full tie-dye. He matches

her gaze, and then quickly glances away. Next Jenny's eyes lock with the dread-locked woman behind him, who glares back at Jenny long after she has gone past. The next Head stares straight through Jenny with burning eyes. The next Head winks at her and shows his teeth.

Why is everyone staring at me? What's wrong with me?

They know. They can tell. I'm acting like such a bitch, and everyone can see it. I'm so uptight tonight that it shows. Everyone else is out having a good time, and I'm just standing here with my back up against the concrete. I'm just standing here, and Jenny's out there dancing and Brad and Andy are down in the front having the time of their lives and I'm standing here in the hallway like a jackass waiting for them.

And everyone's still staring at me.

The slurred, booming music stops for a few seconds, and Jenny can hear — feel — fifty thousand Heads cheering throughout the stadium. Then the music starts again, but Jenny still can't tell what song is playing.

Of course they aren't coming back for me. This was just some sort of plan to dump me. They couldn't wait to get rid of me.

Jenny has the sudden sensation of motion around her. She opens her eyes, and finds herself moving, stumbling through the crowd. Her senses are all screwed up. Her vision is blurry at the edges, but too sharp in the center. The music from inside the stadium and the chatter and laughter from the people around her are drowned out by the ocean roaring in her ears. The best she can manage is to focus on one thing at a time. Ignore all of the people staring at you. Fix your eyes on that column further down the hall, and keep walking until you get there. Then pick another column and keep on going.

Stop staring at me. Stop staring at me. Pick another column and keep on going.

A sudden clarity pierces the cloud of sound around her. She glances over in the direction it is coming from, to her right, and sees open sky through an opening in the wall. The stadium. The concert. She heads in that direction now, stumbling up a ramp, and she comes out into the night.

And the world spins around her.

She is alone again, at the top of a mountain now, the mountain itself sloping away underneath her at dizzying speeds. The universe is huge, immense around her, and she is just a speck lost in it. Tens of thousands of faceless heads swell around her, sweeping away on either side of her, fading in the distance. Even the band itself is falling away, plummeting into unfathomable darkness.

She is left alone there on the mountaintop, the summit like the point of a needle under her feet, the Earth a tiny marble far below. Tens of thousands of faceless heads crowd around her, shouting out to her, roaring like the ocean.

Jenny spins around to rush back down the ramp. A flood of people rise up to resist her, and she feels herself drowning in a sea of arms, legs, hair. She pushes her way through sweat-soaked flesh, ripe and suffocating. Skin and cloth press in on her, choking her ears, her eyes, her mouth.

Fighting for air, she gives one last push against the current, and flies out, suddenly, into open air. Squirted out like a watermelon seed.

The world rages around her. She is lost and alone.

"Hey, are you okay, sister?"

The words echo in Jenny's head, and repeat themselves.

"Hey, are you okay?"

Jenny fights her way up through the blazing colors and deafening sound.

"Can you hear me?"

Jenny's eyes, which have been open all this time, shift and focus. Somehow, she is in a corner of the concrete hallway, curled up on the cold floor, with her head pressed between her own trembling arms.

"Sister? Can you hear me?"

Her eyes focus again, and she sees something shining in the center of her vision.

It is a silver heart, with silver wings outstretched on either side.

She pushes her eyes shut, and then pulls them open again. The winged heart is still there — a pendant on a necklace.

"Hey, sister? Can you hear me?"

The world around her swings back and forth — churning swirls of color.

"What's your name, sister?"

The world spins faster.

"Come on sister. Stop that. The last thing you need is to smack your head on the concrete."

Something warm presses down on each of her temples. The winged heart reappears in the middle of the chaos of the world.

"What did you take, sister? I need to know so I can help you."

Needles snake out and pierce her eyelids, tugging on them. Someone moans.

"Was it acid?"

Her bones are steel spikes. Her muscles twitch and rage. She needs to break free, to run, to fly. Her hands twitch gently.

"You guys go ahead. I'll take her outside."

The ocean pounds in at her ears.

"No, I'll be fine. There's always tomorrow night."

Everyone's staring at me.

"Come on, sister. I've got you."

The world shifts sideways, and races towards her.

"Just close your eyes. You don't need to watch it. Just walk. I'll lead you."

She pushes and struggles against the snake coiling and tightening on her arm.

"I'll lead you, sister. You can trust me."

The winged heart shines up at her, blanching out the liquid universe around her.

"Close your eyes."

She moves through darkness.

88

The world slips past her, slides under her feet.

The ocean subsides.

"Okay, you can open your eyes now."

She opens her eyes, and the world is empty. Her heart races.

"Now just sit back and relax. You're safe here with me."

Something brushes against her cheek.

"Shh. It's okay, sister. It's just me. I've got you."

She is suddenly cold, freezing, and she huddles down into herself.

"That's right, sister. Settle in. Take a deep breath."

She knows suddenly that the object she's staring at is a parked car.

"What's your name, sister?"

Outside. Somehow she's gotten outside.

"Can you tell me your name?"

But Dee —

"Can you hear me?"

Brad —

"Shh. Settle down. It's okay. Settle down. Take a deep breath."

Ice in her lungs.

"The secret to getting through this is to not think about anything. Can you feel this?"

People stroll past them. They're all staring at her.

"Just feel my hand running down your back. You're in Chicago, at Soldier's Field. It's June 23rd, and you're in Chicago."

Oceans of sound and swirls of color.

"You're in Chicago, at Soldier's Field. My name is Lee."

And then darkness.

"It's June 23rd. My name is Lee."

Something brushes against her arm, and she twists away from it.

"Don't lose me now, sister. Look at me."

The world comes clear around her.

"Focus on something, anything. Find one thing to look at and focus on it."

Something shining . . .

"Don't think about anything. Just focus on something, and listen to my voice."

Winged heart.

"You're in Chicago, at Soldier's Field."

Winged heart.

"I'm stroking your back. You are inside your body."

Winged heart.

"It's June 23rd."

Winged heart.

"What is it you're staring at? Oh, this?"

The pendant twinkles and shimmers.

"My brother gave it to me at my first show. I've worn it to every show ever since."

Winged heart.

"Isn't it cool? I've never seen another one like it."

Winged heart.

"You're at Soldier's Field. My name is Lee."

Her throat untightens. Her breathing eases, before she ever even realizes that she's been having trouble breathing.

"It's June 23rd. You're in Chicago."

Winged heart.

"What's your name, sister?"

Winged heart.

"What's your name?"

Somewhere nearby, a woman is laughing.

"You're in Chicago, at Soldier's Field."

A woman is laughing. She walks right past Jenny, laughing and staring and laughing at her.

"What? Are you okay, sister?"

Everyone can see.

"Hey, wait!"

And she is running running away from everyone everyone can see. Everyone can see that she doesn't belong and she just ruins everyone else's good time and she's just someone they bring along when they feel sorry for her and they don't care who they're with and they want someone to laugh at. They want someone to laugh at and they left her alone and it's all one goddamned funny bad joke.

The world is huge around her, and she has a sudden impression of racing through a desert, a ruins, the bodies of the dead lined up in double rows around her. And the survivors struggle past her, and she runs.

Something snakes around her, grabbing her and tossing her to the ground.

Snakes slither over her, winding around her, trying to

91

crush the life out of her.

A snake, slit-eyed, hovers just inches from her face.

Fangs gleaming.

She screams, and lashes out, tearing at it, tossing it away. It wraps around her fingers, clinging, twining.

"Hey, sister! Hold on!"

Wrapped, choking.

"Sister! It's me, Lee! You're okay. I've got you."

And suddenly there are other voices all around her, shouting at her.

"Say, do you need a hand?"

"No, I've got her."

"She looks pretty bad."

"She's really freaking out. What's she on?"

"Here. Here's her shoe."

"I've got her blouse. She really ripped the hell out of it."

"Here, let me help you with it."

"I've got it. Thanks."

Laughing. Staring. They're all staring at her.

"Hold on, sister. Just relax."

"Do you need a hand?"

"No. I think the crowd is really freaking her out. We'll be fine on our own."

They melt back into nothing.

"You're okay, sister."

Something slips over her foot.

"You're in your body. You're in Chicago."

Something tugs at her arm.

"You're at Soldier's Field."

Oh god.

"It's June 23rd, and you're in Chicago."

Oh god oh god oh god oh god.

"Can you hear me, sister?"

Made an ass out of myself.

"Can you hear me? What's your name?"

Oh god. I just want tonight to be over.

"What's your name, sister?"

"Jenny." The word comes out of nowhere.

"Jenny. Nice name. My name's Lee. Can you say that?"

"Lee."

"Good. Where are you?"

"Chicago."

"Where in Chicago?"

Jenny looks around her. It takes her several seconds to recognize the building looming over her. "Soldier's Field. I'm at Soldier's Field. Oh God — the show."

"Never mind about the show, Jenny. It's been over for more than an hour now."

"Over? But . . . ."

"Did you come with anybody?"

Jenny nods. Something warm brushes down her cheek.

"Hey, don't cry there, sister. We'll find your friends. Where did you park?"

Both cheeks now — hot and wet. "I don't know."

"That's okay, Jenny. We'll just stay right here. You're

friends are out looking for you, I'm sure. They'll find us."

Jenny isn't so sure. People stream by all around them, but Dee, Brad, and Andy are nowhere to be seen. As far as Jenny knows, they've left already without her. She sits there on the asphalt, arms crossed tightly over her chest, feeling hollow and wrung out. Every once in a while, a shiver trembles up her spine, and her whole body twitches at once. All she can do is stare into space, and feel Lee's hand running gently down her spine, and listen to Lee's soothing voice.

After another hour, the cops are starting to sweep through the parking lot, trying to clear out all the stragglers. Only then does Jenny hear a familiar voice in the crowd calling out her name.

"Dee?" Jenny calls back, but her voice is too weak to carry very far.

"Is that one of your friends?" Lee asks.

Jenny nods.

"Dee!" Lee shouts out over the other noises of the lot. "Dee! Over here!"

Dee appears suddenly from out of nowhere, scowling cross-armed over Jenny. "There you are," she scolds. "Where the hell did you get to?"

"Be easy on her," Lee snaps. "She's had a rough night."

"C'mon, Jen," Dee urges, ignoring Lee completely. "We've got to get going. Brad and Andy want to go on a liquor run."

Jenny, her head still light and muffled, struggles up to her feet. Lee rises to join her.

94

"Well, I guess I've got to go," Jenny says stupidly.

Lee scowls over at Dee. "Are you sure you're going to be all right?"

Jenny nods. "Thank you, Lee. I really owe you one."

They hug. Jenny feels tears welling up in her eyes again.

"It's cool," Lee tells her. "I'm just glad you got through it okay."

"C'mon, Jenny," Dee whines. "We've got to get going. The cops are clearing everybody out."

Lee lets her go. "Good bye."

"Good bye," Jenny echoes. "Thank you."

"Just take care of yourself."

Dee tugs at Jenny's arm. "Come on!"

And the two of them slip away into the crowd.

"Where the hell did you disappear to?" Dee asks. "You missed one hell of a show."

Jenny nods, but she isn't really listening.

"You were right, by the way. Brad and Andy went down front without us." Dee glances sideways when Jenny still doesn't respond. But it doesn't stop her from babbling on. "I ended up sitting with some really cool guys in the stands. They had some killer weed with them, man. I got so high!"

Jenny lets her shoes scrape a little across the asphalt. She doesn't even feel the impact of her feet on the ground. Everything in her body feels so far away.

But then suddenly she can feel something — feel something brushing against her forearm. Now that she's upright and moving, something has untangled itself from the folds of her blouse, and is slipping down her sleeve.

Jenny stops in her tracks, and brings her hand up to her face. There, hanging from the cuff of her blouse, is a delicate silver chain. The two ends, snapped apart, dangle free.

Jenny reaches under her blouse, where the chain has gotten snagged on a loose thread. She pulls the whole necklace free.

"Oh God, Dee! We've got to go back! We've got to find Lee!"

"What are you nuts?" Dee shoots back. "We'll never find anybody in this crowd. Besides, the guys are waiting for us."

Jenny glances behind her one last time, and then back down at the necklace in her hand.

Hanging from the broken chain is a silver heart, with silver wings outstretched on either side.

FAMILY

Mrs. Mitchell knew exactly what to expect. After all, she'd gone through own her "wild" period herself, back when she was a teenager. She had done it all: smoked marijuana, gone to rock concerts, slept around with any man who seemed halfway decent. It was 1968, after all, and everybody who was "cool" was doing something that drove their parents crazy.

David was the one who had gotten her into all of those wild things in the first place. He was a tall, soulful young man, a student at the nearby university, who wore only ragged jeans and homespun peasant shirts, and who spent his free time reading Charles Bukowski and Allen Ginsberg. His waves of coal-black hair and the fire in his ice-blue eyes captivated her the first time she met him. She slept with him that first night, and the next thing she knew she was cutting school and band practice to spend time with him, in the two-room apartment he shared with an ever-changing number of hippie friends and drug addicts.

But this lasted only a few months. The high school called her mother, her mother called her father, and her father called the police. They locked David and his friends up in jail — and good thing too, because it turned out they were one of the biggest suppliers of illegal drugs in the city.

Ten minutes after the police brought her home that night — timid and apologetic — her father gave her the whaling of her life. An hour after that she was sobbing next to him in the family car, on her way to stay with her father's maiden sister, who lived in a small town a hundred miles away. Under the watchful eye of her aunt, she dutifully finished high school and never strayed from the straight path again. At graduation, her father hugged her for the first time since she was little. "I thought I had lost you forever," he told her.

The question was: what was she to do next? She wanted to go to college, but college was a dangerous place for an impressionable young girl in those days. So her father sent her off to the local two-year college instead, where she majored in the "domestic sciences."

Six months after she graduated, she married John Mitchell, an arc welder in the local union. Her father had introduced the two of them. John was a hard, quiet man, but he was solid, dependable. He never drank, never strayed. He was home every night exactly fifteen minutes after the end of his shift. He ate dinner silently, read the evening paper, and then fell asleep in front of the television. They spent two weekends a year with his parents, two weekends a year with her parents, and the last week of every August camping at Yosemite National Park. All in all, John was a good, stern father to his children, and a supportive husband. They were a happy, healthy family.

Then one day Anne, their youngest, started spending her time with a new crowd of friends. They seemed harmless enough, from what little Mrs. Mitchell had seen of them. But then, from how little she saw of them, she should have suspected something was wrong.

Then Anne started staying out later and later, sneaking into the house after curfew. As far as John knew, this had happened only once, and that was blessing. The one time he had known, Anne went to school the next day with a sprained wrist and a cut across her cheek.

Oh, John was a bit too hard with the children. Mrs. Mitchell knew that. But that was a good thing in the long run, because she knew that she was much too easy on them. She would stay up late at night, sitting in her bathrobe in the darkened living room, rehearsing the lecture she would give her daughter when she finally made it home. But when Anne straggled in, Mrs. Mitchell would be so glad to have her back in one piece that she would just give her a few words of gentle wisdom and send her off to bed. She was too easy on the children. She knew that.

And now it was too late.

If she had just set Anne straight, the way that Mrs. Mitchell's father had set her straight, then Anne would never have run off. It was summer vacation, so Mrs. Mitchell hadn't been keeping as good an eye on her daughter as she should have. One day, Anne simply didn't come home for dinner. She called the parents of all of Anne's new friends, and they all said the same thing: that the whole group had gone to follow some rock band around the country. Everyone had just assumed that she and John had given Anne their permission.

The rock band in question, the Grateful Dead, was some group left over from the Sixties. Mrs. Mitchell had heard of them, vaguely, during her few months with David. So indeed she knew exactly what to expect — she knew, better even than John did, what sort of things their daughter must have been getting herself into. And so they set out looking for her. The private detective had been almost more than she and John could afford, but of course they had no choice. Anne was family. It was as simple as that.

The call had come, finally, just four hours ago. Anne was staying in a cheap motel in the outskirts of Milwaukee, Wisconsin, where the Grateful Dead was scheduled to play a concert the next night. Worse yet, there were at least three other people staying in the room, and at least two of them were men. The detective offered to pick Anne up and bring her back to Chicago himself, but Mrs. Mitchell declined. The detective had done his work well, but in the end this was a family matter. She wouldn't have her baby escorted home like some common criminal. Instead, she left John a note, canceled lunch with her friend Elaine, and took the family station wagon out of town.

She arrived in Milwaukee at sunset. Then, as night grew around her, Mrs. Mitchell drove back and forth on unfamiliar highways at the outskirts of the city, squinting at a page of scribbled directions. Pool halls, bars, and pawnshops passed by her on one side, and the broad expanse of the municipal airport passed by on the other. Mrs. Mitchell was shocked. Even if Anne trusted her new friends — even if her new friends were actually worthy of her trust — this was no place for an innocent sixteen-year-old girl. Anything could happen to Anne in a part of town like this. She could be attacked or abducted or killed and no one would ever know.

Mrs. Mitchell passed the motel three times before she realized that it was the one she was looking for. It didn't even have a neon sign, as any halfway decent motel would. Instead, a hand-painted wooden placard swayed in the wind under a flickering fluorescent light. Mrs. Mitchell pulled into the parking lot and shut off the car. Her head drooped and shoulders slumped as she peered through the twilight at the crumbling building. It was the sort of place where the maids have sticky fingers and the manager has peepholes drilled into the walls. It was the sort of place you never wanted your sixteen-year-old daughter staying at.

Room 12, the detective had said. The doors to all of the rooms were set in the front wall of the building, facing out into the parking lot. Room 12 was on the second floor. Mrs. Mitchell had to climb a creaking wooden staircase to get to it.

Anybody could just walk up to the room any time they wanted to, she thought to herself. A mugger. A rapist.

Any common drunk from the bar on the corner.

She pounded on door to Room 12 as loudly as her tiny fist could manage. There was a slight pause, and then the music on the other side of the door went silent.

"Who is it?"

"Anne's mother. Let me in this instant!"

There was the sound of someone moving furniture inside. Then the door swung open, revealing a young, bleary-eyed young man. Mrs. Mitchell recognized him as one of the many of Anne's friends who had drifted through her home over the last six months. "Paul, isn't it?" she asked.

"Uh huh."

"I want to see my daughter."

"Okay," he said. He was surprisingly agreeable. "Come on in."

"I'd rather that she come out here."

"Well, she's sort of busy at the moment," the boy told her. "You might have to wait a while. And it's much nicer waiting in here than it is out there."

On the long drive out to Milwaukee, Mrs. Mitchell had been picturing this encounter differently: that Anne herself would be the one to answer the door, and that all Mrs. Mitchell would have to do is grab her daughter by the wrist and drag her down to the car. Anne, suitably contrite, would go along quietly. The thought that other people would be involved — that she might have to fight to get Anne away from her so-called friends — had completely slipped her mind.

Mrs. Mitchell lifted her chin slightly. "Fine. I'll come in and wait."

There's no reason to be afraid, she assured herself.

She stepped into the room. As soon as she was inside, Paul closed the door behind her, and then dragged a shabby nightstand across the floor to block the way. Mrs. Mitchell felt a sudden surge of fear, but Paul explained, nonchalantly, "The lock was pretty bad, so we all just felt safer this way."

"Actually," someone else in the room — a young woman — said, "this motel is a whole lot worse than some people led us to believe."

"Sorry," Paul whined back at her. "I did the best I could with the money we had. At least we have a roof over our heads, not to mention plumbing."

Mrs. Mitchell glanced nervously around the room. The young woman who had spoken was sitting on the bed, wearing jeans and a T-shirt and smoking a cigarette. Mrs. Mitchell recognized her as well — another of Anne's new friends, named Marcie. A young man that Mrs. Mitchell had never seen before was sprawled on the bed beside Marcie, wearing nothing but a pair of ragged cut-offs. Another girl, dressed in just her panties and a T-shirt, sat in a chair in the corner with her feet curled underneath her.

"We're planning on checking out in the morning," Paul was saying, "and finding someplace better a little farther from town after the show tomorrow night."

"Where's Anne?" Mrs. Mitchell asked.

"In the bathroom," Paul answered easily. "And you know how long that takes."

Yes, in fact, Mrs. Mitchell did know how long Anne takes in the bathroom. What she didn't know was that this boy knew it too.

Paul pulled a chair forward from against the wall. "Want a seat?"

Mrs. Mitchell shook her head. She focused on the muffled sounds of running water coming through the bathroom door. Then she glanced around her at the other faces in the room. They were all just staring at her. She was making them nervous. They were obviously anxious about what she was going to do, but too scared or too guilt-ridden to ask.

Then her nostrils caught a hint of an old, familiar, long-forgotten odor.

"You've been smoking marijuana!" she cried out, accusingly.

For a second, the entire room went deathly silent. The looks in their eyes said everything.

But then the boy on the bed lifted a dead, half-smoked hand-rolled cigarette into view. "Sure. Want some?"

Marcie slapped him on the shoulder. "Shut up, Drew. Are you crazy? Of course she doesn't want any."

"Uh, Mrs. Mitchell?" Paul asked. He was still standing by the chair he had offered her, rocking nervously from one sandalled foot to another.

"What?"

"What — what can we do for you?"

"I came to bring my daughter home," Mrs. Mitchell answered, a shocked edge in her voice. What other purpose could she possibly be there for?

"Why?" the girl in the corner asked. "Is something wrong? Did something happen?"

Mrs. Mitchell felt the blood rushing up into her face. "Of course, something happened! My daughter ran away, and I've come to take her back!"

The others just glanced at one another. Mrs. Mitchell had the momentary feeling of someone who's just told a joke that nobody understood.

Paul was the first to react. He stormed across the room and started pounding on the bathroom door. "Anne! Anne!" he shouted. "Get your ass out here. Now!"

Mrs. Mitchell winced at Paul's language. It took her several more seconds to realize what was going on. They were all just as surprised as she herself had been. They hadn't known that Anne had run away. Anne must have told them all that she had her parents' permission to go.

Paul and Marcie both turned to Mrs. Mitchell now, explaining everything in unison and at top speed, so that Mrs. Mitchell couldn't make out what either of them was saying. The girl in the chair pulled her knees up to her face and wrapped her arms around her shins. Drew lit up his marijuana cigarette, and that same piney odor filled the room.

It was into this confusion that Anne stepped out of the

105

bathroom, wrapped in one towel and twisting the water out of her ear with the other.

Anne's friends turned to glare at her. Only then did Anne's eyes focus on her mother.

"Mom . . . . What? How did you find me?"

"Never mind that," Mrs. Mitchell snapped. "Get dressed. We're leaving. You're lucky I don't call the police on all of you."

Paul and Marcie started their jumbled explanations again. Drew picked something up off of the bedside table, and carried it and his cigarette past Anne and into the bathroom.

But Anne just stood where she was, dripping water onto the floor.

"Anne, get dressed this instant, or I'll take you home in that towel!"

"I'm not going."

Mrs. Mitchell was sure that wasn't what her daughter had said. "What?"

"I said, I'm not going!" Anne insisted. "You can't make me. And if you do, I'll just run away again, and I'll make sure you can never find me."

Mrs. Mitchell was dumbfounded. Her voice stuck in her throat. "But . . . but . . . you have to go back."

"Why?" Anne asked, taking a step forward, one hand clutching the top of her towel.

"Your father and I have been worried sick about you."

"He's not worried about me at all," Anne countered. "Did

he do even one thing to help you find me? Did he offer to come here with you to bring me back?"

"I didn't ask him," Mrs. Mitchell answered, her voice smaller than she would have liked.

"You didn't ask him because you knew he wouldn't come," Anne returned. "Or, if he did come, you wouldn't be able to control him."

"Anne, please . . ."

"If I come back with you," Anne said evenly, her own voice small now, too, "if I come back with you, he'll just hit me again."

Again Mrs. Mitchell felt her face flush — with anger again, but this time with embarrassment as well. "How dare you talk about your father that way!" she shouted. "Especially in front of strangers!" But then she saw the expressions on the faces of the others in the room. All of them, except Paul, were visibly shocked by Anne's announcement. Anne hadn't told any of them, except for Paul — who, Mrs. Mitchell suddenly realized, was her daughter's lover.

"We can discuss this on the drive back to Chicago," Mrs. Mitchell announced, reaching out for Anne's arm. But Anne just stepped calmly backwards, out of her mother's reach. "Anne. Listen to me. You can't stay here."

"Why not?"

"You're sixteen," Mrs. Mitchell answered coolly. "You're still my legal responsibility, which means you do what I say!" She made another grab for her daughter — more awkward, less certain, this time — and again Anne stepped backwards, out of reach.

"Mom, listen . . ."

Mrs. Mitchell felt the rage boiling in her now. To be disobeyed like this, to be humiliated like this. And in front of all of these ridiculous children. A voice that wasn't hers shrieked from out of her throat: "ANNE ALLISON MITCHELL, YOU LISTEN TO ME RIGHT NOW! YOU DO WHAT I SAY!"

"No, Mom. I won't," Anne insisted, her own voice raising to match her mother's. "I WON'T. YOU CAN'T MAKE ME!"

Before she knew what was happening, Mrs. Mitchell saw her hand lashing out. She caught a handful of her daughter, and pulled.

She looked down at the empty towel in her hands.

Her daughter stood alone in the middle of the room, naked, with silent tears running down her cheeks. Four slash marks, swelling with blood, ran from her throat and across one shoulder.

Marcie just stood there, with her mouth hanging open.

Paul closed his eyes and turned away.

Mrs. Mitchell looked down at her hand. There was blood and skin under the neatly manicured fingernails.

Silently, she handed her daughter back the towel and sank down onto the bed. Anne covered herself and sat down beside her.

"Mom." Anne's voice was unnaturally soft now. "Why did you come after me?"

"I wanted to keep you safe," Mrs. Mitchell answered,

her own eyes filling with tears. "I didn't want you to get hurt."

"If you take me home, <u>he'll</u> hurt me."

Mrs. Mitchell sobbed softly. "Listen, Anne," she said. "I know he isn't perfect. He has his faults. But he's your father. We're a family. We stick together, no matter what."

"No," Anne insisted. "Not no matter what. I don't want him to hurt me anymore. I don't want him to hurt you anymore either, but that's between you and him. But he isn't my family anymore."

Mrs. Mitchell looked up into her daughter's eyes.

Anne indicated the other people in the room with a sweep of her hand. "These people, Mom, these people love me. They care about what I say and what I think. We help each other. We depend on each other. And we never, never hurt one another. These people are my family now. My real family."

Mrs. Mitchell looked around her at the young, anxious faces. They all looked scared, startled by what they had witnessed. But Mrs. Mitchell could tell that they were good people at heart. They all loved Anne. Anne belonged here. They may not be the most moral people in the world. They may be doing drugs, and God knows what else. But at least they won't hit Anne. They won't ever hurt her.

With a sigh, Mrs. Mitchell stood and crossed to the door. Already, Paul had a reassuring hand on Anne's shoulder and Marcie was tending to her wounds. "Goodbye," Mrs. Mitchell said. "Call when you get back into town."

"You're leaving?" Anne asked, genuinely surprised.

Mrs. Mitchell nodded, and slipped out of the room, leaving her daughter surrounded by caring friends, by family.

The next thing she knew, Mrs. Mitchell was in the bar on the corner, sitting in a greasy phone booth covered with graffiti scrawls. The first phone call she made was to the detective, thanking him for his services and closing the account. Then she made a second phone call — a much shorter one — to her husband.

AFTERSHOW

On the day before the concert, Trip, Eddie, and Jeff spend the afternoon wandering stoned through the mall. It's what they've done almost every afternoon that summer, but today somehow it feels different — probably because they spend most of their time bragging to one another about all of the things they're going to do on the lots the next day.

At one point, Jeff wanders into the toy store, and the others stumble in after him. Trip finds himself standing in front of a peg-board hung with frisbees of all shapes, sizes, and colors. It's been a long time since he's owned a frisbee — since before he was kicked out of school even — so he reaches out and grabs the biggest, shiniest one he can find. He compares the price on the package to the collection of coins and crumpled bills in his pocket. The purchase will wipe him out completely, but when he sees that it's one of those glow-in-the-dark numbers he can't resist. Besides, the four of them have enough home-grown weed to sell at the show the next day, so he'll be back in the money again soon enough.

Trip wanders over to the cash register, pays for the

frisbee, and stumbles back out into the mall. He doesn't even check to see if his buddies are following him — he doesn't need to. The three friends never lose one another, no matter how fuzzy-headed they all get. It's the reason they became such good friends in the first place. Trip wanders lost around the mall parking lot for half an hour, finding first Eddie, then Jeff, and then the car.

They drive back to Eddie's house, where they bake the frisbee under Eddie's father's desk lamp all afternoon. Then, when the sun sets, they all get good and toked up, take the frisbee out into the field behind Trip's house, and toss the glowing disc back and forth to one another well into the night.

They're half-way to the stadium the next afternoon when Trip realizes he's left the frisbee at home. But that's all right, because Eddie remembers he's left the tickets back at <u>his</u> house, so they do a U-turn on the expressway and go back for both.

The scene is in full swing when they finally get to the stadium. They stumble off in different directions, down one row and up the next, never straying more than a hundred yards from one another. Selling a quarter here and a half there, they manage to unload most of their stash before the concert begins. Jeff has scored some acid some time that afternoon, so they each drop four hits and stagger into the stadium and up to their seats in the upper deck.

Trip can't really follow the concert all that well once the acid hits. All he can pick out are random, spacey notes

112

here and there, caught up in the solid wall of percussion. And through it all — through both sets and the set break — he stares down at the glowing object in his hand, only half-remembering what it's for.

He is enough in his head for the encore to recognize the song — "Brokedown Palace" — and he stands up with the rest of the crowd, swaying and singing what words he can fake. Finally, as the guitars, synthesizer, and drums reach a crescendo towards the end of a long jam, Trip flings the glowing object up and away from him, into the hungry darkness of the night.

Larry stands with the rest of the tapers, swaying to the music, making as little noise as possible. It's been a nice mellow show — just the kind Larry likes best — and he knows already that this tape is going to be one of his favorites of the tour. Then suddenly a glowing object falls out of the sky, bounces neatly off of a nearby mike with a single, gut-wrenching PING, and drops to the ground at Larry's feet.

Cursing under his breath, Larry picks up the frisbee, carries it outside the taper's section, and flings it as far forward as he can.

Out of nowhere, something flies over Lila's shoulder, grazing her right ear, and bouncing off the head of the guy in front of her. He's too far gone — he and his buddies have been sucking down beers all night — to feel any pain. Lila leans over and picks the frisbee up off the ground. She's tempted to keep it as a souvenir of the show. But she's never up front before — only five rows back! — and she has

113

the sudden urge to try to get the frisbee up onto the stage. It would be almost like having some sort of connection with the band. One of them — maybe even Bobby himself — might even pick it up and take it home with him, which Lila would never forget for as long as she lived.

She screws her eyes shut and — with a quick, secular prayer — hurls the frisbee straight at Bobby's head.

She opens her eyes. The frisbee sails neatly forward, but then it gets caught in a wind current, tilts down, and lands just a few feet short of the edge of the stage.

This is only the second time Mike has been a bouncer at a rock concert. He sure as hell loves it more than working security at the football games, which is probably why all the guys with seniority keep the concert details for themselves. The music is a little loud, of course, and a couple of those kids look as if they're ready to foam at the mouth over the middle-aged jerks on the stage behind him. But something in the air makes him feel light and cheerful, bringing back some fond memories from his own teenage years. A frisbee lands a few feet away from him, and he scoops it up and hurls it back into the crowd.

Frank watches the fuzzy white glow get bigger and closer. It skims off the head of a biker five rows in front of him, and then sails right into Frank's practiced hand. Hmph. A Joy-Toy Deluxe — the glow-in-the-dark model at that. Brand new, too. Hell of a thing to just toss around at a show. It's worth a good ten bucks at least.

As the band lingers over the last few notes of the song,

Frank stuffs the frisbee into his backpack and starts working his way through the crowd and towards the stairs.

It takes him a good twenty minutes to make it from field all the way out of the stadium and back into the main lot. The vending scene is going strong, and Frank wastes no time in joining in himself. He pulls the frisbee out of his pack, holds it up over his head, and shouts out at the top of his voice: "Kind trippy frisbee. Just ten bucks!" Most of the people around him ignore him completely, but it's always that way just after a show. Most of the action right now is people rushing to their cars trying to beat the traffic. In about half an hour the only ones left in the lots will be sellers and buyers. And security guards, of course.

"Buy my frisbee! Just ten bucks! Help me bail a brother out of jail."

Frank starts working his way up Shakedown Street, keeping an eye on the other venders lined up on either side of him.

"Help me bail a brother out of jail! Glow frisbee! Ten bucks!"

"Five!" someone yells out nearby.

"Ten or nothing," Frank growls back, and walks on without waiting for an answer.

"Radioactive frisbee! Ten bucks!"

Then his ears pick out the words he's been listening for: "Cold Sam Adams! Two bucks for a cold Sammy Adams!"

Frank tucks the frisbee under his arm and starts worming his way through the crowd.

115

"Icy cold Sammy Adams! Two bucks for an icy cold Sammy Adams!"

As the voice gets closer, Frank lifts the frisbee above his head once again. "Kind radioactive frisbee! Just ten bucks!"

He spots her finally — a girl in an army jacket two sizes too big for her, standing over a red cooler planted in the middle of the flow of traffic. She's a tiny thing — a good head shorter than the people streaming around her — but her voice is big and she's holding her own in the crowd.

Frank stands near her now, on the side of the aisle himself, calling out his sales pitch in counterpoint to hers, until she finally glances in his direction. He catches her eye.

"Hey, sister," he says, stepping up to her.

"Hey," she answers, looking away.

"How much for a six?"

She turns to face him. "Twelve bucks."

Frank counts a beat for effect, and then shakes his head. "Damn. I don't got the cash. Would you be willing to make a trade?"

"Got any grass?"

"No. How about a frisbee?"

She shakes her head.

"Come on, sister," Frank pleads. "It's brand new. A Joy-Toy Glow-In-The-Dark Deluxe."

The girl shrugs. "I don't play."

"I just bought it yesterday," Frank goes on, although he can feel the deal sinking fast. "I wouldn't be selling it now,

116

except my girlfriend got busted with some weed this afternoon, and she has all my cash."

"Icy cold Sammy Adams. Two bucks for an icy-cold Sammy Adams."

"Four beers?"

"Two bucks for an icy-cold Sammy Adams."

Frank knows when he's beaten. If he had any sense, he'd just go looking for another vender selling Sammies. But as often as he wanders away through the crowd, he keeps coming back to the girl again. He couldn't be more attached to that little red cooler if he were tied to it with a leash.

"Icy cold Sammy Adams," the girl cries out, and Frank's mouth starts watering again.

"Buy my frisbee!" Frank shouts, holding the glowing disk high up above the crowd. "Ten bucks for a frisbee so a thirsty brother can buy himself some beer."

Almost immediately, a heavy-set, blurry-eyed man steps up to him from out of the crowd. "Hell, man," he says, slapping Frank on the shoulder "I'll do anything to help a brother score some beer."

"All right, brother. You're a lifesaver."

"How 'bout five?" the Head offers.

Frank looks up at the frisbee, and then down at the dwindling bottles in the vender's cooler. "Okay, okay. You got a deal."

The Head takes the frisbee and hands Frank a greasy five dollar bill. Frank immediately spins around to the beer vender. "How about three for five?"

Andy tucks the frisbee under his arm and wanders further into the lot. He spends the next hour browsing and shopping and buying, and his arms are soon draped with T-shirts and his pockets are weighted down with necklaces and bracelets. Twice he almost lets the frisbee, still pinned under his arm, drop, but Andy never loses any merchandise once he's bought it. Lord only knows when the Grateful Dead will come through town again, so he wants to get good and stocked up on the sorts of things you can only find at a show.

At eleven-thirty, five security guards — surly men in red shirts — appear at the stadium end of Shakedown and start muscling their way through the crowd, telling the venders to close up shop. They don't chase anybody away so much as push the selling further and further down the aisle, towards the back end of the lot. Andy stays a good ten feet ahead of the line of guards, eying merchandise and haggling prices along the way.

But the mood of the scene has changed. The venders are uptight now, always checking over their shoulders. It takes all the fun out of it. Andy's about to give it up for the night — trying to remember where he parked his car that afternoon — when he passes a tall, bearded man holding up a T-shirt in the wavering light of some other vender's Coleman lantern. On the front of the shirt is a silk-screen of a giant oak tree, with Jerry's face interwoven into the pattern of leaves and branches. As Andy steps up to examine the shirt more closely, the vender flips it. On the back of the shirt is the same tree in winter, stripped of its leaves, the bare branches crisscrossing into the pattern of a Steal-Your-Face skull.

"Sweet shirt," Andy gushes, grabbing the bottom hem with a free hand. "I've been seeing these all over the lots today."

The vender nods proudly. "Hottest shirt on tour. Want one? I was just about to pack it in for the night."

"What sizes have you got?"

"They're all X."

"How much?"

"Fifteen."

"Fifteen?"

The vender flips the shirt back to the front again. "This is a four-color silk screen." He puts his hand under the shirt to bring the design up fully into the light. "Look at the quality of that print job."

Andy shifts most of his merchandise to one arm and fishes his other hand through the pocket of his shorts. "All I have left is ten. Can't you cut me a break, brother? I really want one of these."

The vender glances down at Andy's armload of loot. "Fifteen is the price."

"Could I sweeten the deal with a trade, maybe?"

Again the vender turns a skeptical eye to Andy's collection. "Depends on what you're willing to part with."

It's Andy's turn now to look down at all of the things he's gathered throughout the evening. "How about this frisbee?" he offers. "It glows in the dark," he adds weakly.

The vender shrugs. "What the hell. Last sell of the day."

"Cool!" Andy juggles his goods once more, managing to come up with both the frisbee and a ten dollar bill in his free hand. "Thanks a lot, brother. Have a good one."

Bill shakes his head as he watches Andy waddle away under the burden of his load. Damn tourist.

He slips the ten into the wad of bills weighing down the left-hand pocket of his shorts. By his count, that was the sixty-third shirt he's sold that day. He's made enough money at this one show to cover the whole rest of tour.

And to top it off, he thinks, I got a frisbee in the bargain. It's been a long time since I've toured with one of these.

Self-satisfied, whistling to himself, he slips the frisbee into his backpack. He's about to pull out a fresh shirt to sell, but he stops himself. Looking at the crowd all around him — the river of Deadheads buying and selling, streaming up and down the narrow sidewalk — he decides he's done enough business for one night. So he just hefts the backpack up onto one shoulder and, reaching into his right-hand pocket, he pulls out the clay pipe he traded a shirt for earlier that afternoon.

"Hey," he calls out, "could somebody fix my bowl?"

No takers. Walking along the outside edge of the aisle, he moves a little further along and tries again.

"Hey, could somebody fix my bowl?"

"What's wrong with it?" somebody calls back.

"It won't smoke," Bill answers.

120

"Hey, man," another voice rings out. "I might be able to fix that for you."

Bill follows the voice to one side of the aisle, to a card table stacked with bumper stickers. A woman in a Rasta hat sits behind the table, one arm draped casually but firmly over a grey steel cash box. A man in tattered Guat clothes sits on an up-turned milk crate beside her, his arms thrust between his knees, his hands clutching the insides of his calves.

Bill hands the bowl over to the woman. "You any good at fixing these?"

She smiles back at him. "Come on back here and we'll see what we can do."

"My name's Bill," Bill announces, stepping around the table and settling heavily on the ground.

"I'm Josie," the woman answers, pulling out a quarter-ounce bag of pot. She tilts her head in the direction of the man beside her. "This is Freak."

"Hey, bro."

But Freak doesn't seem to hear either of them. He starts up in the middle of some other conversation. "I've got to score that sheet, Josie. Just one more sheet and I'll have enough to keep me going at least until Christmas."

Josie is digging through the bag, pulling out the occasional stem and seed. "There's hardly any leaf in here, Freak. How much did you say you paid for it?"

"It's good shit, Josie," Freak insists. He's rocking back and forth now. "I got it from Matt."

"Oh, well, <u>Matt</u>," Josie shoots back, rolling her eyes. "<u>He</u> wouldn't pass off any dirt weed on us." She grabs one of the bumper stickers off the table and sprinkles a tablespoon of pot onto the flat surface.

"Wait," Bill offers. "I've got something better for you to clean that pot on." He reaches into his backpack and pulls out the frisbee.

"Cool," Josie says, taking it from him. She spills the pot onto the smooth plastic surface, and uses one corner of the bumper sticker to separate out all of the stems and seeds. She works her way quickly through the pile, with practiced speed.

"You — you sure you want to clean our weed in that, Josie?" Freak asks. "That glow stuff doesn't rub off, does it?"

"Just take it easy, Freak," Josie shoots back.

"How's the vending been going?" Bill asks — anything to stop the two of them from fighting.

"My stickers have been moving pretty well," Josie answers, still bent over her work. "Freak's been having a little trouble with his shirts."

"You have shirts?" Bill asks.

"Yeah. Want one?"

"Can I see?"

Freak unlaces his arms from around his legs and reaches down into the white plastic garbage bag at his feet. He pulls out a couple of muddy tie-dies, all of them shrunk at least a full size.

He holds a few shirts out to Bill, but Bill just nods back at him. Josie breaks the stalemate by loading Bill's bowl with pot and making a flicking motion with her thumb. Bill whips out his lighter, and thirty seconds later all three of them are holding sweet smoke in their lungs.

"Not bad," Bill says finally, and his words come out in a flowing cloud.

Josie nods. "Yeah. Not too bad at that."

They pass a good fifteen minutes that way, smoking and chatting. Freak keeps asking Josie to lend him money, and Josie keeps ignoring him. She and Bill talk about the show — especially the long, haunting "He's Gone" in the second set — until their heads are too light and tingling to hold a conversation.

"Well, I guess I'd better go," Bill announces, slapping his knees and tottering up onto his feet.

"Thanks for the use of your bowl, man," Josie says.

"Thanks for fixing it," Bill answers. He digs one of his shirts out of his backpack. "Here."

Josie holds it up to the light to get a closer look at the design. "Sweet. These are really sweet."

"Yeah," Freak agrees, but he glances at the shirt only for a second.

"Here you go," Josie says, holding the shirt back out to Bill.

"Keep it."

"Cool."

"You guys going to Deer Creek?"

123

"Yeah."

"See you there, then," Bill says. He scoops up his backpack and slips away into the flow of the crowd.

"Just fifty bucks, Josie," Freak continues, without a break. "You know I'm good for it."

"No, Freak," Josie shoots back. She folds up the shirt and slips it into her duffel bag. "You know our deal. Your money is your money, and my money is mine."

"But I'm not talking about taking any of your money," Freak whines. "I'm talking about a loan. One more sheet and I can make it through December."

"No."

Freak backs off for a full ten seconds.

"Lend me the money and I'll split the sheet with you."

"What am I going to do with half a sheet of acid?"

"Hey, wait," Freak says. "I didn't say anything about half."

Two security guards whiz up to the card table in a white golf cart. "Okay, folks," one of them barks. "Time to close up shop and go home."

Josie hasn't sold a sticker in almost an hour. She's all but forgotten that her stand is still set up. She jumps immediately to her feet. "You got it," she tells the man, trying to sound as straight as possible. The guard glares at her to drive the point home and then sputters off to bother somebody else.

The first thing Josie does is lock up the cash box and stuff it way down into the bottom of her duffel. Then she

124

stacks the stickers up as neatly as possible and slips them into the old shoe box she brought them in. She puts out the lantern, folds up the table neatly, but when she reaches down to fold up the chair she's been sitting on something gleams weakly at her from underneath.

"Shit, Freak. Look at this." She pulls the frisbee back out into the night.

"Oh well. I guess it's ours now."

Josie shakes her head. "Nah. He said he'd be at Deer Creek. We'll keep an eye out for him there." She turns the frisbee over in her hands. "And if we can't find him, we can always give it to Tony for his birthday. He'd love one of these."

She stuffs the frisbee into the duffel bag, and then she takes the milk crate back from Freak and puts the lantern and the box of stickers in it. Freak settles down in the grass, watching her pack. Finally, everything is in its proper container, stacked in a neat pile. Josie surveys it all for a few seconds, her hands on her hips.

"It's too much for us to do in just one trip," she announces. "I'm going to take my duffel back to the car first, and then I'll come back and we'll do the rest."

"I thought the table had to go into the trunk first," Freak says.

She looks over at him now, for the first time in hours. Her eyes are first puzzled, then suspicious, and then resigned. "You're right. I'll take the table, and you stay here and watch the stuff."

125

"Okay."

Josie glances back at him one more time, then hefts the card table up onto one shoulder and slips into the dwindling traffic of the aisle.

Freak watches the card table — rising above the crowd like a sail — until it is several hundred feet away. Then he snatches the frisbee from out of the duffel and steps into the aisle himself.

"Kind frisbee. Buy a kind frisbee. Just fifteen bucks!"

He stands there hawking, the crowd thinning out around him. Everyone's heading home.

"Kind frisbee. Buy a kind frisbee. Just fifteen bucks!"

Nobody's paying any attention to him, and Josie will be back any minute now. In desperation, he heads down towards the stadium end of the aisle. There seem to be more people down that way.

"Kind frisbee. Buy a kind frisbee. Just fifteen bucks!"

He's within ten feet of the end of Shakedown when a security guard appears in front of him, his face cut with a crooked sneer.

"Clear out!" the guard orders.

"Just let me sell this, man, and I'll be on my way."

The guard snatches the frisbee out of Freak's hands and tosses it into a nearby pile of garbage. "Clear out!" he repeats.

"Hey, you can't do that —"

The guard grabs Freak by the shoulders and spins him around back in the direction he came from. "Clear out now,"

126

the guard snarls, "before I decide to frisk you."

Freak slinks away. "Fucking Nazi," he grumbles under his breath.

Loner wanders through the crowd, head low, always on the lookout for an opportunity. A grilled cheese sandwich here, half a cookie there — you never know what you're going to find. He jogs right through a drum circle, ignoring the drummers and dancers completely, ducking expertly between legs and around flailing feet. This is Loner's fifth tour, and he knows the scene pretty well by now.

On the fringes of the main vending aisle, he comes upon two barrels side by side, filled with — overflowing with — garbage. It's mostly cans and half-empty beer bottles — the stale smell overpowers everything else. Still, Loner manages to find the remains of an egg roll, and polishes it off neatly, licking the crumpled wax paper clean.

He's about to move on when a weird light catches his eye. Nosing an empty six-pack box out of the way, he finds a battered frisbee, glowing faintly in the darkness. He hasn't played with one of these in months. He grasps it in his teeth and trots away into the crowd.

Along the way, people keep stooping down to pet him. They whistle at him and call out to him as he ducks past. One of them even tries to grab the frisbee away. Loner breezes past it all nonchalantly, keeping his head down and his eyes forward, pretending not to notice any of it. He keeps his nose to the ground, carefully sampling the smells.

In one of the back aisles, he catches sight of the low red

light of a fire. As he comes closer, he picks up the mixed scents of charcoal, beans, and grease. The man behind the table is busy talking to the man in front of the table. They're arguing about something, and neither of them is keeping an eye on the burito baking on the grill. Loner drops the frisbee by the wheel of a parked car and slips through the shadows and around behind the vender.

When the vender turns away to take something that the other human offers him, Loner puts his front paws silently up on the table and gently snatches the burito off the grill.

But the other human sees him. "Hey, would you look at that!"

"Christ!" the vender shouts. "Give me that!" He makes a move to grab the burito back, but Loner growls and starts backing away.

"Let him keep it," the customer says.

The vender reaches into the bag sitting next to him and pulls out something small and round. The next thing Loner knows, a lump of charcoal whizzes right past his ear. Another one quickly follows, hitting the ground at Loner's feet.

"I'll pay for it, man," the customer is saying. But Loner has already turned tail and scampered away — off to a sheltered spot between two parked cars, where he can enjoy his meal in peace.

Allison is exhausted. It's been a long day for her. It's the first time she's ever brought Joey to a show, and it's proved to be more work than she'd originally thought. Still, with that cotton stuffed firmly in his ears, Joey did seem to enjoy the concert. She'll make a Deadhead out of him yet.

She's pushing him along through the parking lot, trying desperately to remember where they parked, when a faint glow catches her eye. It's a frisbee, sitting in a puddle off to one side of the aisle. She picks it up and dries it off with the tail of her shirt. It's her first ground score ever, even though she's been touring for years now. And what a ground score it is!

She walks back over to where she left Joey, leans over and touches him lightly on the shoulder. He stirs a little, shifting in his seat. Allison slips the frisbee under his arm, and he shifts again, cradling the disk to his chest. He looks so peaceful, sleeping there in the middle of all of this chaos. It's been a long day for him too.

Allison admires his passive face, brushing a hand through his fine blond hair.

Then she straightens back up again, and they continue on their way. She's pushed the baby stroller only another few feet when she catches sight of her car, waiting patiently for them under the flicker of a dying streetlight.

ABOUT THE AUTHOR

Alex Kolker got to celebrate both his 25th and 30th birthdays by attending Dead concerts. He also had the mixed pleasure of seeing Jerry's last show in July of 1995. One of his few regrets in life is that he turned down the chance to see the 7/6/90 show in Louisville, Kentucky, which is now one of his favorite bootlegs.

ABOUT THIS BOOK

You may obtain additional copies of this book at the following address:

Sinister Dexter Press
PO Box 916
Kewanee, IL 61443-0916

or by e-mailing us from the link on the following web page:

http://home.earthlink.net/~amylex/ToT.html

The cost is $7.50 per book, which covers the price of the book itself as well as the postage.

Sinister Dexter Press has also been known to supply copies of this book free of charge to Heads under the care of the United States Penal System.

Printed in the United States
1260800001B/163-210